Women in India

Women in India

Negotiating Body, Reclaiming Agency

Metti Amirtham, SCC

RESOURCE *Publications* • Eugene, Oregon

WOMEN IN INDIA
Negotiating Body, Reclaiming Agency

Resource Publications
An Imprint of Wipf and Stock Publishers
199 W. 8th Ave., Suite 3
Eugene, OR 97401
www.wipfandstock.com

ISBN 13: 978-1-60899-621-6

Manufactured in the U.S.A.

Dedicated to My Beloved Dad
Late Mr. Amirtham

Contents

Foreword ix
Preface xiii
Acknowledgments xv
Notes on Transliteration xvii
Glossary xix
Introduction xxiii

1 Mapping the Boundaries 1

2 Laying the Foundation and Constructing a Theoretical Framework 17

3 Socio-Cultural Perceptions of the Female Body 38

4 Reclaiming the Body, Beauty, and Sexuality 87

5 Female Agency: Negotiating Embodiment 116

Appendix I—Survey Questionnaire 133
Appendix II—Profile of the Respondents of Quantitative Data 143
Select Bibliography 147

Foreword

IN 2006 I EXPERIENCED what was to become for me a turning point in my theological journey. Along with more than 400 colleagues I participated in the First Meeting of Catholic Theological Ethicists in the World Church. That conference provided unparalleled opportunities for meeting colleagues dedicated to a Catholic approach to questions about the moral life—the human life of striving for what is true and good—in the contexts of local and global realities of pain and suffering, comfort and hope, and work done and yet to be done. From the plenary sessions of the conference we learned with no uncertain argumentation that women suffer indignities in disproportionately greater numbers and more brutally across nations and cultures. If I had any misgivings about focusing my own attention on the vulnerability of women those misgivings were then and finally dispelled.

In addition to the insights gained from the conference I was inspired to find a way to collaborate with the women present and their colleagues at home. Earlier in that year I was involved in a panel discussion on HIV/AIDS that proved to be the subject hook for a collaborative project. I gathered the names and contact information of 50 women whom I knew were involved with studies regarding the pandemic or about whom other colleagues directed me. I wrote a mass email to them all, inviting them to contribute an essay to *Calling for Justice throughout the World: Catholic Women Theologians on the HIV/AIDS Pandemic* (Continuum, 2008), a companion collection to *Catholic Ethicists on HIV/AIDS Prevention*, edited by James F. Keenan (Continuum, 2002). *Calling for Justice* includes twenty-five essays by women from Africa, Asia, Europe, North and South America, and Oceania; and Metti Amirtham, SCC, PhD is among them.

The turn on my journey, then, was not only toward the experiences and concerns that women have regarding many subjects related in whole or in part to theological ethics. The turn was also toward collaboration and developing relationships with women and men who share a commitment to specifically Catholic approaches to the moral life and the moral questions of conscience, justice, and peace in local and global contexts of corruption, poverty and food and health security, and violence. Finally, the turn included a firm intention to mentor junior colleagues in the field by creating opportunities for presentation and publication of their work.

I was humbled and honored when Metti Amirtham asked me if I would write a foreword to her book. I had invited her to be the speaker at Barry University's annual bioethics lecture and to speak about the discrimination against and discrepancies in the access to and degree of healthcare extended to women in India. I also had the opportunity to meet her at the Annual Meeting of the Society of Christian Ethics (January 2010, San Jose, CA), where we spoke about the importance of attention to the human body, in female form, in order to respond to the concrete expression of solidarity with the women of her homeland, Tamilnadu. I thought about my turn in theology to recognize that she and this work exemplify what I had hoped to do. Finally, as I reflect upon this work, I am even more humbled by the breadth, the implications, and the passion she here brings to bear.

Earlier in my academic career I had studied the history of the Indian subcontinent and its religious traditions, going so far as to learn the ancient language of Sanskrit and to read some of the Hindu scriptures. I was enamored with the land and its peoples; I was drawn to the metaphysics and the yogic practices, and intrigued by a vegetarian diet. When I became acquainted with the teachings of Mohandas Gandhi I was even more interested in the ways of ahimsa peace. And then my naïveté about that fabled land was exposed when I looked to the experience of the people, particularly of those assigned as Dalit untouchable, that reflected the multiple violences and indignities of abuse, poverty, illiteracy, gender and class discrimination. I remain devoted to the people and the cultures of India and I am hopeful that those who are marginalized and/or otherwise oppressed will find their voice and allies so that they too will flourish in the land.

I will not rehearse the hard realities faced by far more people than most of us in privileged contexts realize and which our author, Metti Amirtham, will introduce. As you read the text you will be able to better appreciate both the common threads of the oppression of women throughout the world and the unique vulnerabilities of women in India as well as reasons to be alarmed and to work for a change in the circumstances that continue to degrade our sisters. The principal focus of the work is, in the end, about the incarnation—the embodiment of meaning-making, to borrow the author's use of phenomenological studies, and self-reflection that leads to and affirms empowered moral agency.

Moral agency is one of those terms about which much thinking in philosophy and theology is concerned. The moral agency with which Amirtham is concerned belongs expressly to the women whose ability to determine the course of their lives is severely restricted and who even here find a way to assert their dignity, however much it may yet be denied by others. However and sadly, this restriction is not limited to the women and culture of Tamilnadu. It is the widespread denial of women's agency in many parts of India, elsewhere in Asia, Africa, Central and Latin America as well as in Europe and North America—in effect, everywhere—that is told and re-told in the accounts of Ponmalar, Kokila, Parvati, Kaajimujja, Eswari and others included in the book, which cries out for justice and the rediscovery of the God-given gift that is the body where the theology of another incarnation and its embodied agency is possible.

Finally, this work provides a critically engaging examination of how women's bodies reveal the meaning that the powers of this or that dominant culture, in this case, that of the patriarchal heritage of traditional Asian and western cultures, assign to themselves. This point, that the ways in which those who are "the least among us" are perceived by those who "other" them, exposes their own fears about non-conforming/non-hegemonic and abnormal secrets they harbor about themselves. That all of us, dominant and oppressed alike, should recognize these fears can be among the first steps required in programs and theologies to reverse the damaging and damning systems that deny agency to those whose lives and livelihoods depend on its free and rightful exercise and whose sacredness, power, and beauty—whose treasure—refuses to be hidden or buried but shines for all to see and rejoice.

Mary Jo Iozzio, PhD
Co-Editor, Journal of the Society of Christian Ethics
Professor of Moral Theology, Barry University

Preface

Theology can become quite futile and even irrelevant if it does not emerge from a context and from the day-to-day lives of the people. A theology that does not pay attention to the experiences and views of the ordinary cannot make a stronger and deeper impact. Moreover, theology, on its part, has to be answerable to the church and society and fulfil its noble mission of contributing towards the transformation of the present order of the church and society. This book is ultimately aiming towards this. By identifying the ideological underpinnings that emerge from the perceptions of women, this book indicates possible future directions in the area of theology.

The uniqueness of this book lies in its contextual focus and the day-to-day lived experiences of women with their bodies. It is the first of its kind in making a scientific study on the socio-cultural perceptions of women with regard to their bodies in the Indian context. The special contribution of this book is in bringing to the fore the elements of *agency* which women exercise in their everyday lives in spite of their oppressive situations.

This book comes as a boost to women who are oppressed while at the same time challenging thoroughly the patriarchal attitude of the oppressors of women. The unconventional women of this book become possible role models for women who are voiceless, helpless and victimized to grow in assertion and affirmation of their bodies and identities. Hence this book will certainly contribute in bringing awareness among women who hate their bodies because of oppression / misuse / abuse by their husbands, lovers, fathers and society. It will facilitate women to deconstruct the age-old oppressive perceptions and construct their identity as women in relation to their bodies and to take hold of their bodies amidst dehumanization.

The book will also facilitate a critical look at the present understanding of body in Christian theology and provide future directions for the reformulation of the Theology of Body and Sexuality. This book will help orient and strengthen the action-plans and strategies of NGOs and Self-Help Groups to enable women to take control of their bodies.

This book would be of great help to scholars and graduate students in Gender studies, the NGOs, Self Help Groups, Policy makers, feminists and all those men and women who are truly concerned about the empowerment of women and the establishment of equality at all levels of the church and society to initiate the process of women exercising bodily empowerment and agency.

Metti Amirtham SCC
Tamilnadu

Acknowledgments

THE BOOK HAS EMERGED out of my interest and involvement in the lives of women for their empowerment. Ever since the feminist consciousness has engaged me, I am aware of the various ways in which the body becomes the site of women's oppression. Hence, it is my concern and conviction to contribute towards the emancipation of women.

However, without the help of those who stood by me and backed me up sometime or other, during the period of my research as well as during the editing of this book, it would have been impossible to see the completion of this book.

First of all, with deep sense of gratitude, I raise my heart to *God*, the Creator of the 'human body' who imprinted in it *His own image and likeness* and has breathed *His life* into it.

At the outset, my sincere thanks go to the women *participants of this present work* in the area of Dindigul district, Tamilnadu who willingly shared the secrets of their lives concerning body. It is their flesh and blood that fills the pages of this book.

I express my profound appreciation and gratitude to my congregation of *the Sisters of the Cross of Chavanod* for their unflagging support in this endeavor of mine and for giving me the time, finance and the space required for this venture.

It is indeed a rare privilege to have Professor and Head of the Department of Christian Studies, University of Madras, India *Rev. Dr. Fr. Felix Wilfred* an internationally well-known theologian, as my guide and supervisor of this task. He has played a remarkable role in the shaping of the project by his frequent reminders, insights, and suggestions to make me more analytical and critical in my approach.

I owe a special debt of gratitude to the faculty of the Department of Christian studies, University of Madras, for their generosity and interest towards my work by giving me their valuable suggestions.

Very special thanks to *Rev. Dr. Michael Amaladoss SJ*, who painstakingly commented on, revised and edited my final script in minute detail. I am very grateful to him for all the help that he has rendered selflessly towards the birth of this book.

I am deeply indebted to *Fr. Alphonse Prabhu* for he has played a very decisive role in standing by me from the time of its conception till its completion. His persistent motivation and prayerful support spurred me on to go beyond the hurdles that I encountered in this journey.

Finally, with deep sentiments of joy and gratitude I recall with love, the unceasing warmth and the emotional and prayerful support *of my loving parents, my sisters Sr. John Marie, Jeya, Saro and Roseline and my brother Jerry and their family members.* They have helped me to understand and face the agonies and the ecstasies of this work. In a special way, I fondly remember my dad, *Mr. Amirtham*, with love, though physically not with me today, he continues to be part of my life. In fact I dedicate this work to him who taught me to how to listen, respect, and respond to my body. I am deeply and sincerely indebted to Wipf and Stock Publishers who have given space for the voice of women in India, be heard by publishing my work. Words are inadequate to express my deep sentiments of gratitude to all There are some who have been placed on record here, while many others, whose names are not mentioned here, have also contributed to the completion of the book. I remain immensely indebted to each and every one of them.

Notes on Transliteration

METHOD OF TRANSLITERATION FOLLOWED in this study is taken from the Tamil Lexicon, published by University of Madras in the year 1982. Cf. *Tamil Lexicon,* Vol. I, 1982, ixviii.

All Tamil words, except the names of persons, places, hills, mountains and rivers that are in present usage, are transliterated and italicised. Names of gods and goddesses are transliterated but not italicized.

The common Sanskrit words such as *shakti, varna, moksa,* etc.... are not transliterated but italicised. As a rule, the non-English words found in **quotes** or titles of works are given in their original form and not transliterated.

அ	ஆ	இ	ஈ	உ	ஊ	எ	ஏ	ஐ	ஒ	ஓ	ஔ	ஃ
a	ā	i	ī	u	ū	e	ē	ai	o	ō	au	k̲
க்	ங்	ச்	ஞ்	ட்	ண்	த்	ந்	ப்	ம்	ய்	ர்	ல்
k	ṅ	c	ñ	ṭ	ṇ	t	n	p	m	y	r	l
வ்	ழ்	ள்	ற்	ன்	ஜ	ஷ	ஸ	ஹ	Ñ	ÿ		
v	l̲	ḷ	r̲	n̲	j	ṣ	s	h	kṣ	ś		

Glossary

Āttā—A way of addressing a Hindu Goddess

Alaiyātē—Do not long for sex

Accamum, maṭamum, nāṇamum, payirppum niccamum peṇpārkkuriyatu—Fear, ignorance, shyness and sobriety are all qualities of women.

Alayiṟā pāru—She is longing for sex

Amaṅkali—A woman who is inauspicious

Ammā—Mother

Aṭakkam—Modesty and docility

Aṭaṅkāppiṭāri, Ōṭukāli—A loose woman

Cittāḷ—A coolie involved in construction work

Ciṉṉa vīṭu—A concubine

Cumaṅkali—A married woman whose status is auspicious status as opposed to a widow whose status is inauspicious.

Cīmantam—Celebration during pregnancy

Cilappatikāram—One of the Tamil epics

Kaṭalai māvu—Flour of black gram

Kallāṉālum kaṇavaṉ pullāṉālum puruṣaṉ—Even if he is a stone, he is your husband.

Kaṟi—A leaf used for cooking while seasoning any curry items

Kaṟpu—Chastity

Kaṟpu Aḻiñcu pōccu—She has lost her chastity

Kaṟpukkaraci—Queen of Chastity

Kaṉṉi tīṭṭu vīṭṭukku ākātu, Kaṉṉi tīṭṭu kaṭavuḷukku ākātu.- T—the impurity of the virgin is not good for the family and for God.

Kaṟuppi Or Karuvācci—A girl with a dark complexion

Kuṭumpa kauravam—Prestige of the family

Kāttu kāṟuppu—The spirits of those who have died with committing suicide or else those who have been killed or those who have died with unfulfilled desires

Lakṣmaṇa-rēka—A line of Laksmana

Malati—A Barren Woman

Mañcaḷ—Turmeric powder

Muḻugāma Irukkā—A woman who is pregnant

Muṉi—The Spirit of the dead person

Māmiyā vantuṭṭā—Mother-in-law has come

Māta viṭāy—Menstruation

Māta vilakku—Bodily isolation or separation of a woman during monthly menstruation.

Meṭṭi—Toe ring

Nāṉ tīṭṭā irukkēṉ—I am impure

Nāṉ cuttamā illai—I am not clean

Pati viratāi—Wifely fidelity

Paruvam tavaṟiṉāl paṉaṅkiḻaṅku nārākip pōyviṭum—If the season is lost, the pulp of the palm will become a fibre.

Peṇ pārkkum paṭalam—It is a visit of the boys' family to see the girl and her family before marriage.

Periya manuṣi āyiṭṭā—She has become a sexually mature woman.

Pēy vativu—Form of a Demon

Pompaḷa ciriccā pōccu: pokayila viricca pōccu—A laughing woman is equal to tobacco which has lost its essence by opening out.

Puruṣaṉa muntāṉaiyile muṭiñcu vaccukkō—Tie your husband in your sari.

Purāṉā(s)—Sacred narratives of Hindus

Pūja—Prayer

Pūppuṉita nīrāṭṭu viḻā—Celebration for Puberty.

Peṇṇukku vīṭu tāṉ ulakam: Āṇukku ulakamē vīṭu—For a woman, the home is her world; whereas for a man, the world is his home.

Rāmaṉ irukkum iṭamē Cītaikku Ayōtti—Sita's destiny is wherever Rama is.

Summā tānē irrukirāi—You are sitting at home without any work.

Tīrkka cumaṅkali—Eternal bride

Uṇṭi Curuṅkutal Peṇṭirkkaḻaku—It is beautiful for a woman to eat very little

Tāimai aṭaital—To attain the state of motherhood

Tāimaiyē peṇmai—Motherhood is womanhood

Tāli—A sacred chain or thread which the husband ties around his bride's neck on the day of wedding.

Tīṭṭu—Impure

Tōṭṭam—Farm

Vaṇṇāṉ—Washerman/woman

Vaṇṇāṉ māttu—Exchange of clothes provided by washerwoman

Veṭkam—A sense of shame

Vīṭṭukku tūramā irukaa—She is distanced from the house

Vīṭṭukku tūramā irukkeṉ—I am away from the house

Introduction

LOCATING THE SUBJECT

MANY SHOCKING INCIDENTS IN which women's bodies are violated reveal the harsh realities of women in India today. Right inside homes, in public places and in globalized markets, women's bodies are victimized and degraded. Moreover, in the Indian context, the female body seems to have no value unless it is adorned with jewels, flowers, costumes, and so on. Attractive as it is, the female body is perceived as beautiful and unclean, alluring and dangerous, a source of pleasure and a cause of shame and a spring of renewal and a power of destruction. All the same, at the academic level, there is a dearth of books on the female body in gender studies in India. Following are the features of the context within which the present book is set.

The Reality of Female Body in India Today

Zahida, a 32 year old married woman, was blinded, her earlobes chopped off and her nose cut off by her husband for 'dishonoring' him by having an alleged affair with a brother-in-law. He avenged the injury to his 'honor' by tying her hands and feet and gashing her face with a razor and knife while she pleaded that the allegations were false. He did not stop. She survived somehow, just short of getting killed. She was three months pregnant at the time.[1]

In one of the remote villages in the district of Raipur three women who had lived almost 40 to 42 years of their married life were accused of being witches by the entire village. Thus, they were beaten, given electric shocks, stripped, head shaven and finally they had to drink urine in the presence of more than 250 men. And this went on from ten in the morning until six in the evening on 21st of October 2001.[2]

1. Shirin, "Wombs," 22.
2. Sail, "Witch Hunting," 47.

The magazine *Frontline* reports another incident. During the Gujarat riots from February 28—March 3, 2002, women were the target of sexual violence. They were gang raped, mutilated and then burnt to death. While making his comments on what happened during the Gujarat carnage, the then Union Minister, George Fernandez, said: "There is nothing new in the mayhem let loose in Gujarat. A pregnant woman's stomach being slit, a daughter being raped in front of a mother is not a new thing. Such things have been happening for 54 years in India and have happened even in the streets of New Delhi in 1984."[3]

These are some of the cruel realities of domestic and communal violence against women's bodies in India.[4] Besides, women's bodies are abused by information and communication technology, viz., through television programs, newspapers, magazines, internet websites, etc. Women are expected to reduce their bodies in size and shape in order to fit the standard of the mass media.[5] Woman's body is openly exposed and sold like hot cakes for profit.[6] Social issues like abortion, pornography, rape, and new technologies of reproduction have guaranteed a continuing, perhaps eternal, controversy about the rights and violations of the female body.[7]

3. This remark, which was made in Parliament on April 30, 2002, was reported by many dailies in India.

4. Shocking statistics on what is done to women's bodies reveal the precise picture of India. A woman is raped every 54 minutes, two girl children are raped every day, one woman is killed every 102 minutes in the name of dowry, half of the women are married below 18 years of age, every year 10, 000 female fetuses are denied life and nearly 30 million agriculture women workers receive wages below the minimum wage limit. Women form nearly half of the human population but their body is treated as the weaker sex in all societies of the world, not getting their due in any field. Women do two-thirds of the work, earn one-third of the national income, but own only one-hundredth of the property. The representation of women has never crossed 10 percent in the *Lok Sabha* (it is a Hindi word which stands for the House of the People, directly elected lower house of the Parliament of India) and in the State assemblies. The affirmative action to rectify this in the form of Women's reservation Bill is still pending. Hundred percent of women's income goes for family survival as compared to the partial contribution of male incomes. Female illiteracy is one-third more than male illiteracy. Girls' drop-out rates are higher. Violence against women and children is growing, as minor girls constitute almost thirty percent of all victims of sexual assault cases. Conviction rates are below ten percent in all cases of atrocities against women. Cf. Nandal, "Laws Inadequate," 34.

5. Wong, "Menstruation," 7.

6. Sinaga, "Women Claiming," 14.

7. Wong, "Menstruation," 7.

These few illustrations reveal that there has been a history of incidents of repeated injuries and insults to woman's body in spite of the progress and contribution that women have made in every field.

Female Body in Academia

The female body, as Margaret Atwood[8] remarks, is a 'hot topic' for authors and scholars in the West who have produced a large amount of research in the last two decades in order to situate the female body in the diversity of historical and theoretical contexts.[9]

As a significant outcome of the United Nations Decade for Women, several researches were conducted in India; so too many publications were made. Feminists like Kamala Bhasin, Nighat Said Khan, Madhu Kiswar, Gabriele Dietrich, Gail Omvedt, Aruna Gnanadason, and Vandana Shiva and others have broached woman's question in their own ways. They believe that the patriarchal system is a deep-seated cause for the exploitation and oppression of women. A number of books are available on the economic development strategies needed for women's empowerment. However, in the area of the female body, books are scarce.

In the current Indian context, a significant work on the body is by David Arnold, entitled *Colonizing the Body*. He emphasizes the importance of 'the body as a site of colonizing power and of contestation between the colonized and the colonizers.'[10] Vandana Shiva's work shows us the crucial links between the body and nature, between the 'earth body and the human body through the processes that maintain life.'[11] Kalpana Ram's *Mukkuvar Women* and Karin Kapadia's *Siva and her Sisters* are written against the background of rural South India, more specifically, from the context of Tamilnadu. In 1997, Busby made an attempt in this area by making an ethnographic study of Mukkuvars in Kerala. She has brought to light the indigenous ideas of the gendered body.

Meenakshi Thapan's book on *Embodiment: Essays on Gender and Identity*[12] is a collection of essays providing analysis of everyday life, in

8. Atwood, "The Female Body," 1.

9. Goldstein, *The Female Body*; Shilling, *The Body*; Bordo, *Unbearable Weight*; Suleiman, ed., *The Female Body*; Isherwood, ed., *The Good News of the Body*; Grosz, *Volatile Bodies*; Jeffreys, *Anticlimax*.

10. Arnold, *Colonizing the Body*, 7.

11. Shiva, *Close to Home*, 3.

12 Thapan, ed., *Embodiment*.

different contexts, spaces, locations and historical settings, all seeking to articulate nuanced understandings of the relationship between embodiment, gender and the constitution of identity. The thrust of these essays is on the 'body as a social construct' as well as the 'lived body' of every woman's experience in her daily life. It seeks to understand and explicate woman's body, both in its material and representational aspects, and in the context of different social, cultural and historical settings in contemporary society. In one way or the other, all the essays address questions relating to inequalities, which are revealed in the complex interplay between society, gender and body in everyday life.

Seemanthini Niranjana in her book on *Gender and Space*,[13] which is an anthropological discourse on woman's body, seeks to address what she considers the two major axes that define woman in specific socio-historical contexts, viz., 'femininity (as an acquired attribute), and its grounding in the female body.' Seeking to take an account of both the biological and the cultural in the formation of gender identity, Niranjana examines the 'situated' female body, in 'space, time and culture.'

Besides, some anthropological studies in the Indian context[14] highlight how woman's embodiment and her sexuality serve as important boundary markers of the cultures or religions to which they belong.

Feminist activists have, perhaps more consciously than others, addressed the *gendered* aspects of social behavior, exploitation and violence in relation to the female body, rape, domestic violence, sexual abuse, and health-care.[15] Journals like *Manushi*, *Women's Link*, and *Sakhi* speak of domestic violence and other issues that concern women. Nevertheless, by and large, in the Western and Indian feminist researches, attention has been focused on the oppression and marginalization of women. Researchers have not gone into the lives of women to see *how they perceive* and deal with their bodies. There is also a general silence on how women exercise their agency to take control of their own bodies in the patriarchal society.

13. Niranjana, *Gender and Space.*

14. See for example, Bennett, *Dangerous Wives*; Fruzetti, *The Gift of a Virgin Women*; Mandelbaum, *Women's Seclusion*; Ganesh, *Boundary Walls.*

15. I am referring to the different feminist groups and organizations in India, who are actively involved in the documentation and dissemination of knowledge on issues relating to women's embodiment in very many different ways. Also, see Gandhi and Nandita, *The Issues at Stake*, chs. 3 and 4; Dietrich, "Discussing Sexuality."

Growing Perception of Human Body

There has been a growing interest in bodywork and body-management. Far from the Platonic negation of the body, it is today fore-grounded in a person's life-plan in a unique way. There has also been a steady growth of popular interest in the body. Doubtless, one of the main features of contemporary life-style is the preoccupation with the body.

Newspapers, magazines, television and websites are replete with features on body image, plastic surgery and tips to keep the body young, slim, sexy, and beautiful. In fact, the business of weight-loss and keep-fit is now a multi-million dollar industry. To be young, to be beautiful, and to be fit are the goals for good and successful embodiment.

Furthermore, the place of the body within contemporary popular culture reflects an unprecedented *individualization* of the body. People are increasingly concerned with the health, shape and appearance of their own bodies as expressions of their individual identity.

However, the increase in the purchasing capacity of people and the available options has turned body-management into a 'body cult,' promoting the commercialization of health. In conditions of high modernity, there is a tendency for the body to become central to the modern person's sense of self-identity. What Pierre Bourdieu[16] noted in 1980s about the concern that was prevalent, and especially acute among the `new' middle classes, has spread, in recent years, beyond the narrow confines of the middle classes, to those who are economically in the lower rungs of society.

Besides, in recent developments in the areas of biological reproduction, genetic engineering, plastic surgery and the science of sports, the body has become increasingly an object of options and choices. The body is seen as an entity that is in the process of becoming; a project that should be worked out as part of a person's self-identity. This necessitates a practical recognition of the significance of the body, both as a personal resource and a social symbol. In this respect, the way in which the body has become a project for some women would appear to be more reflective of male designs and fantasies than an expression of individuality. Therefore, there is a need to venture into research as to how women feel with regard to their bodywork and body-management.

16. Bourdieu, *Distinction: A Social Critique.*

Challenges of Feminism

Feminism[17] has, from the beginning, been deeply concerned with the body—either as something to be rejected in the pursuit of intellectual equality according to a masculinist standard, or as something to be reclaimed as the very essence of the female. It has long seen its own project as intimately connected to the body and has responded to the masculinist convention by producing a variety of incompatible theories, which attempt to take the body into account.

Yet, what is overlooked in most of these feminist theories is how women reclaim their bodies and become acting subjects of their own history. The present study resonates with the stance of postmodernist feminism that seeks to emphasize the importance of *embodiment* as a differential and fluid construct, a site of the potential, rather than as a fixed given. This book makes a contribution in the area of feminist studies, bringing to light through a field study in the area of the female body as *agency* among the women of Dindigul district, Tamilnadu, India.

In addition to all these, the book has emerged out of my interest and involvement in the lives of women for their empowerment. Ever since the feminist consciousness has engaged me, I am aware of the various ways in which the body becomes the site of women's oppression. Hence, it is my concern and conviction to contribute towards the emancipation of women.

Besides, the Christian approach to body has been ambiguous down the centuries with an emphasis on its negative aspects. The body has been considered as an evil and a cause for sin, whereas the soul has been considered as pure and higher. Lisa Isherwood and Elizabeth Stuart aptly observe that Christian tradition reveals a complex and constantly shifting relationship with the body, going back to the roots of Christianity. The present book, based on an empirical study made in the district of Dindigul, Tamilnadu, India could lead to the kind of a theology that will serve the cause of women.

17. From 1890s, the words 'feminine', and 'feminism' have been used as terms for the politics of equal rights of women. The word feminism can also stand for a belief in sexual equality combined with a commitment to eradicate sexist domination.

Focus and Objectives

The focus and the objectives of this book could be spelt out as follows:

1. Exploring the differing socio-cultural perceptions of women with regard to their bodies.
2. Studying the exercise of women's *agency* in the perceptions of their bodies.
3. Inquiring into the factors leading to differing perceptions among women regarding their bodies.
4. Highlighting the implications and challenges posed by these perceptions to feminism in general, and feminist theology in particular.

Hypothesis

I had the following hypothesis while making the empirical study: There is a small segment of women in Dindigul district , Tamilnadu, India who think and act differently and go against the existing socio-cultural perceptions of their body. The enunciation of this hypothesis enabled me to be more open to the participants' perception of their body during the course of the field study.

Organization of the Book

The book has five chapters. A brief description of its individual chapters is presented here below.

The first chapter sets the background of the socio-economic and cultural universe and condition of the women of Dindigul district, Tamilnadu, India, along with the general outline of the district of Dindigul, its physical and geographical layout. The second part of this chapter presents the demographic profile of the women respondents.

The second chapter clarifies the key terms and concepts of the title frequently used in the book. It also presents the method of enquiry and implementation and discusses the theoretical framework of the book.

The third chapter phenomenologically presents the self-perceptions of women regarding their body, at different phases of their lives. The various themes that are covered in this book are space, motherhood, menstruation, beauty, chastity, sexuality and labor. The data collected are coded, categorized and grouped together to delineate the various factors in women's perceptions of their bodies. They are: the perceptions of the respondents, the underlying attitudes of these perceptions, the elements of agency in the perceptions and the supportive factors of the respondents.

Chapter four presents the hermeneutical interpretation made among the significant findings of the data to further the meaning of agency found in the women respondents, taking into consideration their patriarchal context. From a broad framework of contemporary feminism and using concepts, arguments and insights from Indian and Western feminists, this chapter also argues how agency acts as a key and matrix of this border-crossing and that reclaiming of women's bodies is disclosed in these elements of agency.

The first part of fifth chapter presents the main findings and conclusions of the book, while highlighting the three salient contributions of the thesis, regarding methodology to feminism and feminist theology in India and Asia at large. And the second part attempts to propose from a feminist point of view some theological reflections and implications derived from the findings.

Conclusion

Having introduced the topic, relevance, objectives, hypothesis and the structure of the book, I now proceed to present the socio-cultural universe of the research area, namely, Dindigul district in Tamilnadu, India along with the socio-cultural conditionings of women respondents and their demographic profile.

1

Mapping the Boundaries

CHOICE OF THE SITE

One day, while I was travelling in a bus from Dindigul to Oddanchatram in Tamilnadu, India, a man was trying to molest a woman vendor who happened to stand near him with a basket of flowers. As soon as the woman realized that he is abusing her body, she turned towards him and slapped him forcefully. The bus came to a halt immediately. While all the travelers' attention turned towards her, she walked out of the bus fearlessly with her head held high. This incident shattered my perception of women for a moment. The other women who were seated next to me informed us that women here would thrash men if they misbehaved with them.

Generally, in a patriarchal society like India, when a man abuses a woman's body either in private or in public, she simply tolerates it and does not make a scene out of it. Nevertheless, this woman behaved differently. What made her do that? How or from where did she get that courage? These questions kept returning to my mind. I wanted to know and study more about the women in this district and to explore how they perceive and deal with their bodies. Hence, among the 29 districts in Tamilnadu, India, I undertook to make an enquiry among the women of *Dindigul District.*

SETTINGS OF DINDIGUL DISTRICT

The socio-economic and cultural background plays a significant role in determining the individual's perceptions, attitudes, and behavioral patterns. In order to understand the worldview of the respondents, these pages endeavor to set the background for the field, namely the socio-economic and cultural universe of the women of Dindigul district.

The first part of this chapter attempts to sketch the general outline of the district of Dindigul and an overview of the situation of women. The second part presents the demographic profile of the respondents of the research area, which was collected through a questionnaire survey.

Physical Layout and Geographical Milieu

Approaching from Madurai, a huge rock emerges on the horizon like a *dhindu*, which means 'pillow,' hence the name Dindigul. Known as one of the ancient historical cities in Tamilnadu, Dindigul was under the sovereignty of the famous Muslim Monarch, Tipu Sultan.

Dindigul district was carved out of the composite Madurai District on 15th of September 1985. It was formerly named after one of the illustrious sons of Tamilnadu, the late Mr. C. N. Annadurai who was popularly called *Anna* (an endearing term for elder brother in Tamil), and the district was formerly called Anna District, but is now called Dindigul District.

Location of the State of Tamilnadu in India

Map of India

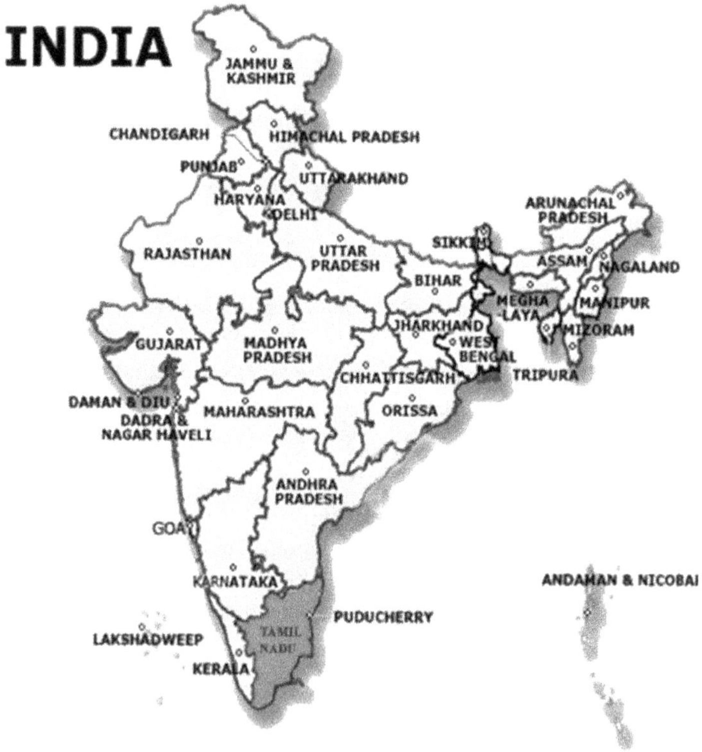

LOCATION OF DINDIGUL DISTRICT IN TAMILNADU
MAP OF TAMILNADU

MAP OF DINDIGUL DISTRICT

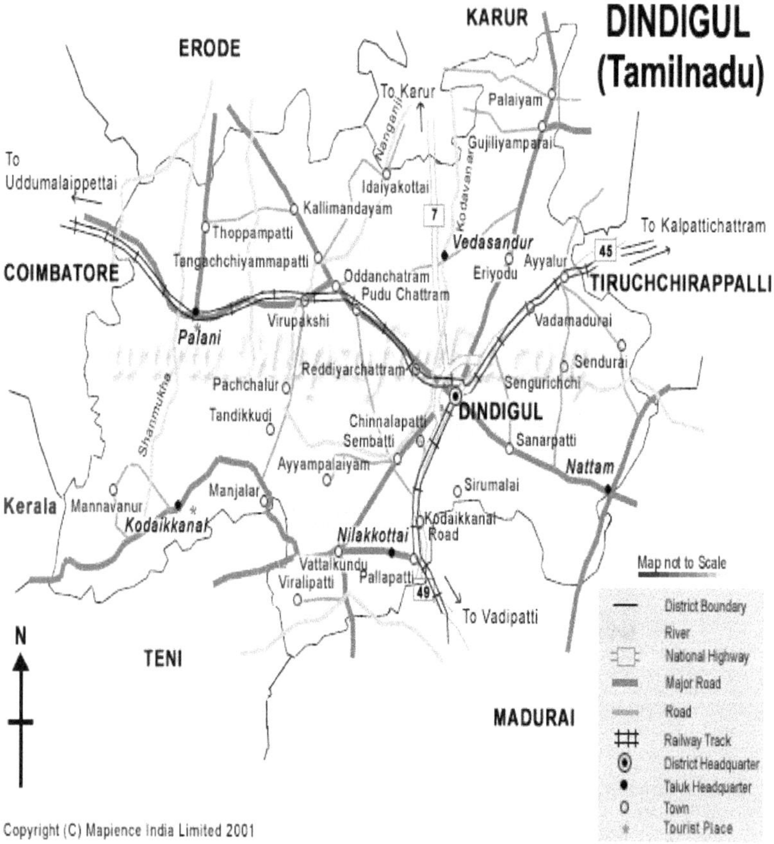

The district spans an area of 6,266.64 square kilometers. It consists of a section of the plain stretching from the eastern slopes of the Western Ghats. The district is surrounded by Karur and Tiruchirapalli districts on the North, Sivagangai district on the East, Madurai district on the South, and Theni and Coimbatore Districts and the State of Kerala on the West.[1] Considerable portions of the district are covered with lovely hills. There are also a number of isolated hills and rocks in the district. The principal river of the district is Vaigai. It flows through the district and meanders into the neighboring district of Madurai. Dindigul is also called one of the "forest belts" of the state.[2]

1. For the social survey of Dindigul District, online: http://www.dindigul.tn.nic.in/default.htm. Accessed on 15.04.2003. See also Raj, Dindigul Anna District at a Glance, 30–34.

2. *Tamilnadu–An Economic Appraisal 2001–2002*, 56.

The district consists of three Revenue Divisions, 7 Taluks, and 14 Panchayat Unions. The three revenue divisions are Dindigul, Palani, and Kodaikanal. The seven Taluks are Dindigul, Kodaikanal, Natham, Nilakottai, Oddanchatram, Palani, and Vedasandur. This district incorporates 24 semi-urban areas and small towns, 358 hamlets and 304 village panchayats. Fourteen *panchayat* unions have authority over the town and village panchayats.

Agriculture is the linchpin of the economy of the district, especially in terms of creation of employment, since the soil of Dindigul district is fertile. Dindigul and the surrounding taluks are known for the cultivation of onion and groundnut. The taluk of Kodaikanal is well-known for the cultivation of potato,[3] apple, tomato, carrot, beet-root, and other highland vegetables as well as for its varieties of fruits and flowers. Plantain, jackfruit and lemon are cultivated in Sirumalai hills. The taluk of Oddanchatram is known for the cultivation of cauliflower, tomatoes, etc. The taluk of Nilakottai is known for the cultivation of flowers, especially jasmine. The other crops like rice, sugarcane, maize, grapes, groundnut, and cereals are cultivated in other parts of the district.

Dindigul city, which is an important wholesale market for onion and groundnut, has a network of inter-district roads connecting Coimbatore, Erode, Tiruchirapalli, Karur, Madurai, and Sivaganga districts.

Though there are many riverbeds in the district, only occasionally one finds water flowing in these rivers. For irrigation, the district depends entirely on monsoon rains. Since the rainfall in the district was not good during the past years, the yield rate is at a low level. This has resulted in ever-increasing poverty in this district.

The Dindigul District is devoid of any major industries except for a few leather industries. However, there are 65 cotton mills in and around the district. It is considered as one of the few pockets in Tamilnadu with a high concentration of leather tanning units. Of Tamilnadu's 568 tanneries, one-fifth is located in Dindigul District, which generates employment to more than 3,000 persons, half of whom are children.[4] For a long time, Dindigul town is also associated with manufacturing iron locks and iron safes of high quality and durability. Its renown for lock manufacturing is next only to Aligarh in the country.

3. http://www.dindigul.tn.nic.in/kodai.htm. Accessed on 12.04.04.

4. Shanthi, "The Impact of Tanneries," 272.

The widely known *Angu Vilas Scented Tobacco* and *Roja Supari* produced in this town are sent for marketing to various places in Tamilnadu and outside. In addition, the district has a flourishing handloom industry at Chinnalapatti, which is located 11 kilometers from Dindigul on the Madurai-Dindigul Road. Art-silk *sarees* and Cuṅkuṭi[5] *sarees* produced in Chinnalapatti are famous throughout India. There are more than 1,000 families engaged in this industry. Besides, there are a few small-scale industries like beedi-making, weaving, etc.

According to the 2001 Census,[6] the total population of Tamilnadu is 62,405,679 and out of it, the male population is 31,400,909 and the female population is 31,004,770. Dindigul district has a population of 1,923,014. Among them 968,137 are male and 954,877 female. The district has a rural population of 1,249,762, whereas the urban population is only 673,252.

The district is composed of people who belong to different social categories. Within each village, the central part is occupied by castes comparatively higher in the social hierarchy and scheme of economic dependence (like *Vanniyars, Kallars, Aasaaris, Udayars, Gounders, Mudaliyars, Thevars, Nadars*, etc.). The scheduled castes and tribes inhabit the fringes of the settlement. The *vanniyar* community is predominant in the district and other communities are a small minority. The scheduled castes and scheduled tribes number only 376,170 and 6,484 respectively.[7] However, a peaceful lifestyle is mostly found among the different caste groups.

A breakdown of the joint family system is taking place in the country. Majority of the families in the district are nuclear families. In addition, social education and the consequent awareness created both by the media and the non-governmental organizations have played a positive role in making people accept the small family norm. Generally, people here live in tiled houses. However, people of poor economic conditions live in thatched houses, and those economically well off live in houses with concrete roofing. In the semi-urban areas and towns of Dindigul district, most of the people still maintain the traditional lifestyle of the villages. However, the impact of technology and modernization has not left these places unaffected either.

5. Cuṅkuṭi *sarees* are made specially Madurai and Dindigul districts.
6. Cf. *Census of India 2001*- Demographic Atlas of Tamilnadu, 3, 29.
7. Cf. *Census of India 2001*.

The district has 3,226 high and Higher Secondary Schools. In addition, there are nine Arts and Science colleges, 5 institutes of Engineering and Technology, 2 colleges for Special Education, and 5 Schools for professional education. There are two Universities, viz., Mother Theresa University for Women at Kodaikanal, and Gandhigram Deemed Rural University, specializing in studies on Gandhian principles and way of living.

SOCIO-ECONOMIC AND CULTURAL CONDITION OF WOMEN

Having traced the contour of the district under study, we now move on to understand the socio-economic and cultural condition of women in the district in general.

Reign of Patriarchy

In the social sphere, whether they are in cities or in rural areas, there are clear evidences of patriarchal dominance in the district. Women are treated as secondary citizens. The conditions of rural women are far worse than those of urban women. Men mostly decide matters concerning women. Women have status neither in their parents' homes nor in society. A woman is told just to do what she is asked to do, and remain dependent on others. The social system controls women in such a way that she has no other choice except to submit herself to patriarchal values.

Declining Female Sex Ratio

Despite the overall improvement in the sex ratio and literacy in Tamilnadu, *The Hindustan Times* reports:

> The female infanticide belt stretches through the districts of Salem, Dharmapuri, North Arcot, Periyar, Dindigul, and Madurai. The hardcore regions are in North Salem, South Dharmapuri, South Dindigul, and West Madurai. These blocks accounted for practically 70% of all female infanticides in Tamilnadu in 1995, according to the Primary Health Centre records. The survey also revealed that female infanticide was not confined to the Kallar community in Madurai and the Gounders in Salem. It was prevalent among 35 'self-ascribed' caste groups in Dindigul and the Thevars, Vanniars, Pariyars and Pallars in other areas.[8]

8. *The Hindustan Times* (New Delhi, October 11, 1996), 3.

The deplorable conditions of women due to dowry problems, mounting expenditure for marriages, unemployment, failure of agriculture because of continuous drought and other natural calamities have forced them to get into such a heinous practice as female infanticide. This was confirmed by Sudha, one of the field workers and a member of a NGO, who said, "Women kill their baby girls quietly without the child's birth is being brought to the notice of the public."[9] Due to the impact of female infanticide and infant mortality in Dindigul district, there is a steady decline in juvenile female sex ratio.

Rapid Increase in Crimes

Crimes against women in the district are also on the increase. According to the police records and reports for the year 2000, there were 20 rapes, 4 dowry-related deaths, 51 molestation incidents, 58 kidnappings, and 22 incidents of eve-teasing.[10] In 2003, we notice an increase in the number of crimes perpetrated against women. There were 208 rapes, 66 molestation cases, 158 dowry deaths, and 287 other heinous crimes against women.[11] These are only the recorded cases. Many cases go unregistered either because of a fear of threats by the opponents or because of a sense of public humiliation.

The Educational Situation of Women

Although the district has a good number of educational institutions, it is unfortunate that the literacy rate of the district is below the average for the state. The literacy level of women is remarkably low. The total literacy rate of the district is 69.3 percent: 79.8 percent male and 58.9 percent female literates. The gender gap in literacy is 20.9 percent. Women laborers continue to remain in unorganized sectors due to this reason also.

Women and Employment

The Work Participation Rate is one of the indicators by which one can measure the absorption of female labor in the total employment force.

9. Personal communication with an NGO worker in Vathalagundu on August 12th, 2003.

10. Jeyaseeli, "Gender Based Crimes," 115.

11. Information received from the District Police Station, District Crime Records Bureau, Dindigul, 02.12.2003.

The total number of workers in Dindigul district is 973, 332. Among them 585,146 are male and 388,186 are female.

The Work Participation Rate for males increased from 56.58 percent in 1981 to 58.96 percent in 2001, whereas for women it rose from 26.53 percent to 31.32 percent.[12] Women in the district are engaged in different types of work. Most women in hilly areas and in villages involve themselves in plantation work, while the educated women are more often than not involved in the teaching profession. Only a few women are involved in white-collar jobs.

The District Census of 2001 reports that there are only 385,108 female workers among the female population of 952,759. By the arrival of the new economic policies of liberalization, women experience a new atmosphere of freedom and the possibilities for upward mobility. More and more women in rural and in suburban areas go to work in unorganized sectors, but they are at a disadvantageous position because they lack either proper skills or educational qualifications. They are employed as daily wage earners depriving them of the benefits of permanent employees, which would entail them to dearness allowances, provident fund, medical benefits, maternal leave, bonus, etc. Most of the women employed in tanneries and mills in and around the district have put in more than ten to fifteen years of service, but can make no claims to gratuity or any monetary or other benefits as in well-organized factories. However, women form a large portion of the unskilled labor force,[13] due to acute poverty at home.

The women-workers in this district are mostly involved in the cultivation and distribution of flowers, vegetables, and fruits. Their work takes them to neighboring towns for the sale of flowers or vegetables and fruits, increasing thus their physical mobility.

The deficit rainfall, experienced during the past years (2001–2004), has largely affected the lifestyle of the farmers, by landing most of them in long-term unemployment and depriving them of the necessities of life. As a result, they are without safe drinking water, firewood, and fodder for their cattle. Women suffer more because they are mostly responsible for the water, firewood, and fodder for their cattle. They have to walk miles and miles on an uneven path in the countryside to collect water, firewood, and fodder.

12. Ibid. Cf. also *Women in Tamilnadu—A Profile.*

13. Ibid.

In addition, there are other socio-economic problems such as unemployment and poverty, lack of social and economic infrastructure. Consequently, women face much oppression and repressive violence because of their dire poverty at home.

The Health Condition of Women

Women in this district are known for hard work and are exposed to harsh conditions of life. All the same, the health-care system is discriminatory against women. During pregnancy and childbirth, women are faced with many diseases related to their reproductive organs. Most of the rural women suffer from acute infections, which frequently lead to tuberculosis and cancer. The ill-treatment by husbands and the social system is the cause for these infections and they do not have adequate basic amenities. They also fall victim to HIV/ AIDS.

Women and HIV/AIDS

Escalation of women victims of HIV/AIDS is a recent phenomenon in the district. The enchanting tourist centre—Kodaikanal—that invites thousands of people from different states and from different lifestyles throughout the year turns also its neighboring towns like Dindigul, Vathalagundu and Nilakottai slowly into flesh-trade zones. Since they are at the foothills of Kodaikanal, there are hotels meant for prostitution without attracting public notice. Since Kodaikanal is a very cold place and it is quite expensive for middle class men to hire a room in a hotel there, they prefer hotels in Vathalagundu and Dindigul for their sexual gratification. Besides, Vathalagundu and Dindigul are marketing centers not only for the locality but also for the states of Tamilnadu and Kerala as well.

The tourists and merchants flock to these towns every day, and especially during the summer. Variety of vegetables and fruits are brought for sale from the rural areas as well as from the high ranges. Hence, frequent arrival of drivers of lorries and trucks of all sizes and tourists into this district leads to abuse of women. According to the information provided by one of the local hospitals,[14] 10–15 women HIV patients visit the hospitals daily for treatment. The number is on the increase. The infection of the reproductive tract of women is also high in these areas.[15]

14. This information was collected from Leonard Hospital, Vathalagundu, Tamilnadu on 15.04.2005.

15. Cf. Soundariya, "Rural Dalit," 22.

Women and Miscarriages

The tanning industry poses a grave danger to the health of the workers. It causes devastation of the agricultural land and pollution of water by chemical effluents. The women workers are especially involved in the most polluting stages of the tanning process. Of the total number of women workers in tanning and its related industries, 66% are engaged in tanning operations, which are most polluting.[16] They have to clean the hides of cattle with acids and chemicals. Thus, they inhale the dust from the hides and their health is affected deplorably and irremediably.

According to the survey conducted by Peace Trust, a voluntary organization, which has been spearheading the campaign against the hazardous effects of the tanning industry, there were 134 miscarriages and 75 stillbirths within a year in Dindigul taluk alone.[17] Adding financial and mental burden to their misery, women have to meet their medical expenses on their own, i.e., from their scanty wages.

Women in Voluntary Organizations

Tamilnadu has entered a new phase of social consciousness stimulating voluntary action, and a number of organizations have sprung up in the recent past. These organizations and associations continue to grow and serve the rural masses by creating awareness among them.18 The influence of action-oriented groups on women is an important factor in Dindigul district, because it has the maximum number of SHGs, NGOs and other movements in the state of Tamilnadu. There are nearly 4,500 voluntary organizations, movements, NGOs[19] and SHGs[20] working in the district.21 These organizations are mostly local and tightly knit, with a focused agenda. They have adopted multifarious strategies to empower women. I observed that a good number of women are part of an NGO or a SHG or a movement. For convenience sake, from now on, in this

16. Shanthi, "The Impact of Tanneries," 273–74.

17. According to the Report of *PEACE TRUST* (An NGO working for the preservation of ecology), Dindigul, 2002.

18. Mowli, ed., *Role of Voluntary Organizations*, 28.

19. NGO stands for Non-Governmental Organization.

20. SHG stands for Self Help Groups.

21. When the author was doing field work in Dindigul district, it had the maximum number of SHGs, NGOs and Movements in Tamilnadu. The period of field work was between 2003 June–2005 March.

book, I use the term 'action-oriented groups.' This term would include voluntary organizations, movements, NGOs and SHGs.

What emerges from the above mapping of the district and the situation of women may be summarized as follows: Dindigul district has been formed by bifurcating the erstwhile Madurai District. The main occupation of the district is agriculture, especially cultivation and distribution of vegetables, fruits, and flowers. The district is considered as one of the most backward districts in Tamilnadu. Women are mostly involved in unorganized sectors. They have to withstand the worst of the family chores. A good number of women are members of SHGs and NGOs that are active in the district.

DEMOGRAPHIC PROFILE OF THE RESPONDENTS

The socio-economic background as a part of the total environment plays a significant role in determining the attitudes and behavioral patterns which, in turn, affect the individual's perception and activities. This part of the chapter seeks to present the demographic profile of the 150 respondents chosen from Dindigul district. They are classified according to religion, age-group, educational qualification, occupational positions, economic level, nature of the family, caste, the area in which they live, their participation in action-oriented groups, and the frequency of the use of the media.

Religion

Religion has been playing throughout the ages a dominant role in the process of socialization and in maintaining the stability of the social system and social relationships. This is very true of the role of religion in Tamil society. The predominant religions practiced by the people of Dindigul District are Hinduism, Christianity, and Islam. Of the 150 respondents 37.8 percent are Hindus, 37.2 percent Christians and 25 percent Muslims.

Age Group

Age is one of the important aspects in the present study. Therefore, women respondents are divided into three groups. The first category of the respondents is in the range of 21 to 30 years; the second category falls within the 31 to 40 age-group; and the third belong to the 40 to 45 age-group. In terms of percentages 28.2 percent of them belong to the age-group of 21 to 30; 37.4 percent belong to the age-group of 31 to 40, and 34.4 percent to the age-group of 41 to 45.

Educational Qualification

The level of education is another important variable that determines one's perception. Therefore, the respondents are divided into four categories based on their educational qualifications, in order to identify the variations in their perceptions. I have placed the illiterates in the first category; women who have completed their primary education (classes 1 to 5) in the second category. In the third category, I have placed women who have completed their secondary education (classes 6th to 12th); and in the fourth category, women who have completed their graduation/post-graduation. 35.2 percent of them were illiterates; 25.6 percent of them had completed their primary schooling; 22.2 percent their high schooling and 17 percent had completed their graduation.

Occupation

Another important variable for judging perception is the occupation of the respondents. The women respondents were classified into three groups based on their occupations namely those employed in organized sectors, in unorganized sectors and the unemployed.

Organized women workers are those who are permanently employed; their job tenure is long; they receive statutory provisions like adequate wages, dearness allowance, housing rental allowance, transport allowances, medical benefits and other facilities. They are also known as confirmed employees.[22] They mostly work in banks, schools, hospitals, factories, offices, etc.

Unorganized women workers include those who cannot be defined, but could be described as those who have not been able to organize themselves in pursuit of a common objective because a) they are scattered; b) the nature of their work is casual or seasonal; c) they are mostly ignorant and illiterate; d) they work in small size establishments with low capital investment per person employed; and e) the power of the employer, operating singly or in combination, is strong. [23] Unorganized

22. Rao, *Women*, 85.

23. Ibid.

women consist of coolies, vendors, cittāḷ (construction workers), domestic servants, and those employed in income generating works. The last group of women is those unemployed, namely the housewives (home-makers). Among the respondents, 21.4 percent are organized workers; 37.6 percent work in the unorganized sector; and 41 percent remain house-wives.

Economic Status

Income is another important index of the socio-economic status of an individual. The women respondents are classified as a group belonging to the poorer section of society (total income of the family below Rs. 2,000 ($43) per month); lower middle (total income of the family between Rs. 2,000—Rs. 5,000 ($43—$107) per month) and middle class (total income over Rs. 5,000—Rs.10, 000 ($107—$213) per month). 29.2 percent of them belong to the poorer section of the society; 26 percent belong to the lower middle class; and 44.8 percent of them are of the middle class.

Nature of the Family

In all societies, whether primitive or civilized, traditional or modern, rural or urban, family remains a vitally important element in social structure.[24] The respondents were categorized according to their family system. The first category of women belongs to the single family, formerly known as a nuclear family, wherein a single parent or both parents are employed and care for their children. The second category of women belongs to a joint-family which has two or more adult earning members, other than the husband and wife. 70 percent of the women belong to the nuclear family, whereas 30 percent belong to the joint-family.

Domicile

There are 358 tiny villages and 304 village *panchayats* in the district. The women respondents selected for our study were both from rural and urban areas, covering all the 7 taluks of the Dindigul District. 52.8 percent of the respondents were from the rural setting whereas 47.2 percent were from both urban and semi-urban settings.

24. Ibid., 52.

Caste

Another variable of the socio-economic background is the caste of the respondents. Caste is known to be a unique institution of Indian society. In fact, Indian society is graded and arranged according to the caste system. The respondents interviewed belong to different castes. However, they all fall under Backward Castes (BC), Most Backward Castes (MBC) and Dalits. 32.2 percent of them are BCs, 43.1 percent are MBCs and 24.7 percent are Dalits.

Involvement in Action-Oriented Groups

As noted earlier, Dindigul district has the maximum number of SHGs, NGOs and social movements in the State of Tamilnadu. To know the impact of these action-oriented groups in the self-perception of women, it was essential for me to know whether the respondents were part of any women's movement or a NGO or any self-help group. Among the respondents 63.6 percent were part of action-oriented groups, whereas the rest had no idea of these groups.

Frequency of the Use of the Media

The media has become part and parcel of human life. During the visit to the research areas, I observed that women do watch Television regularly. The Television is their greatest entertainment. Even those women who do not possess one seem to watch Television in their neighborhood. In order to know their frequency in viewing the media channels, the participants are categorized as women who view daily, once a week, rarely. Among the respondents 24.6 percent of them view Television daily, 46 percent view it once a week especially on Sundays, 29.4 percent view it rarely and there was no one who never views Television. This shows that the media is an integral part of their lives.

Although the main research method is only qualitative, 500 women have been given a questionnaire in order to quantify and strengthen the qualitative findings in the field. The respondents of the qualitative method also form part of these 500 respondents. The break-up of the 500 respondents chosen for quantitative study are presented in tables in Appendix-II. They are classified according to their religion, age group, educational qualification, marital status, occupational positions, economic status, nature of the family, caste, the area in which they live, their participation in a movement / SHGs, and the frequency of the use of the media.

CONCLUSION

This chapter has delineated the contours of the Dindigul district, its geography, socio-economic and cultural situation. It has also presented the overview of the socio-economic and cultural situation of women in the district. The latter part of the chapter has sketched the profile of the respondents under study.

Having studied the socio-economic and cultural universe of the women of Dindigul district, I now proceed to clarify certain concepts, the method of enquiry and theoretical framework of the research.

2

Laying the Foundation and Constructing a Theoretical Framework

HAVING SET AND LEARNT the locale, chapter two moves on to position the underpinnings for the book, by clarifying its basic and recurring key terms, the method of enquiry and the theoretical framework in order to create a better understanding of the book.

CLARIFYING TERMS

Socio-Cultural Perceptions

Every decision and response in a given situation discloses how one is greatly influenced by the social and cultural norms and perceptions of the society. Mostly, perceptions are created by a human society which is bound together for self-maintenance and self-perpetuation, and for sharing their own institutions and culture. Nonetheless, these perceptions differ from individual to individual due to a variety of personal, socio-economic, and cultural differences.

For example, age, gender, race, past experiences and learning, attitudes and interests, needs and feelings, and the current situations affect one's perception. Besides, socio-economic factors namely occupation, level of education, environmental factors, family upbringing and cultural factors, which include language, customs, belief systems, and historical perspective also play an important role in one's perception. Our perceptions are also influenced by the ways our bodies are structured to receive and process stimuli from the environment.

In this process, culture plays a vital role with regard to the formation of perceptions of ideas, values and customs of a particular community. Often these learned perceptions through a process of socialization identify and distinguish the members of a cultural group from another.

Perception also comes from internalization. Especially, in the case of women, the beliefs and values, which come through religious, cultural and political socialization, shape their conduct and behavior and guide their functioning. In the socialization process, the beliefs and values, which shape the behavior of women, are gathered by sense organs, get interpreted as definite meanings and take the form of perception.[1]

The Body

As the book revolves mainly around the theme of the female body, clarity in our focus concerning the body in general and the female body in particular is necessary. Generally the body is defined as the physical or material frame or structure of a human being or of any other animal—the whole material organism viewed as an organic entity. Some of the well-known early anthropologists used the body as a central construct in describing social relations and symbolic systems.[2] For instance, Mauss indicates the body as the first and most natural tool of man [sic].[3] Levi-Strauss explains the body as the total system of social relations, bound up with the system of the universe.[4] In this book, although I focus on to the living physical body of a person, I do not dichotomize the body and the spirit, but understand the body as physical, material as well as spiritual.

Feminine vs. Female vs. Feminist

Very often, terms like feminine, female, and feminist are misunderstood even by the scholars in gender studies. Hence I attempt to clarify in order to bring about a right understanding of these terms.

In reality, the terms *feminine* and *female* have become so intertwined that it is often impossible to see the *female* as separate from the *feminine*. The *feminine* is often perceived as the primary characteristic of womanhood—the factor which determines the social code of conduct

1. Arjunan, *Psychology of Learning*, 53.

2. Cf. Douglas, *Natural Symbols*; Durkheim, *Suicide*; Levi-Strauss, *The Elementary Structures*; Mauss, "Techniques of the Body,"; Turner, *Religion*.

3. Mauss, "Techniques of the Body," 75.

4. Lévi-Strauss, *The Elementary Structures*, 168–69.

for women. *Feminine* qualities are considered a natural consequence of being a *female* by birth. But Simone de Beauvior had raised the issue of *female* and *feminine* and emphasized the distinction between a biological condition (the female) and a socially imposed concept (the feminine).[5] We treat *feminism* as a political position, *female* as a biological term and *feminine* as a set of culturally defined characteristics.[6]

The Female Body

The 'body' is the starting point for feminist concerns and analysis. The reasons for this are many, but the most significant one is that a woman's life is seen as inextricably tied to her body. In a biological sense, a "woman" ordinarily is a person whose chromosomes (XX), internal and external sexual organs and hormonal chemistry mesh in such a way as to warrant the label "female" at birth. This biological "woman" is a human being capable in various phases of life of menstruating, gestating and lactating.[7]

However, the rich variety of social arrangements that exist in the world suggests that biological sex alone cannot explain the differing gender roles assigned in these societies. Beyond the biological core, a woman's body in the social sense is a great many other things, depending on which society we are studying. In this sense, woman's body is a social construct. The emergence of feminist consciousness has brought in a new awareness defining the female body for what it is. The term 'female' is defined as 'one' sex, determined by biology and anatomy.[8]

The female body in this book is viewed as the live body or the communicative body through which a woman seeks to both define her life spaces and express herself in different situations and contexts in everyday life, all of which shape her identity as a feminine being.[9] It is an enquiry into 'the living-body' in the everyday lives of women.

5. Beauvoir, *The Second Sex*, 32.
6. Toril Moi also defines these terms in this way. Cf. Moi, *Sexual/ Textual Politics*, 45.
7. Rao, *Women*, 4.
8. Bechtle, "Theological Trends," 124.
9. See Thapan, *Embodiment*, 44–49.

Feminism

Feminism does not derive its conceptual base from any single theoretical formulation. Therefore there is no specific abstract definition of feminism applicable to all women at all times. The definition does differ because feminism is based on historically and culturally concrete realities and levels of consciousness, perceptions and actions.

All the same, we shall see some of the definitions given by feminists. According to Patricia Meyer Spacks, feminism is an approach that assumes the centrality of woman and seeks to project and interpret experience from the viewpoint of a feminine consciousness and a feminine sensibility.[10]

In the Indian context, Kamala Bhasin and Nighat Said Khan define feminism as an awareness of women's oppression and exploitation, which is at work in society and within the family. It also includes conscious action by women and men to change the existing oppressive situation of women.[11]

Many feminists of today would go by Sandra Schneider's definition of feminism, "as a comprehensive ideology, rooted in women's experience of sexual oppression, which engages in a critique of patriarchy, embraces an alternative vision for humanity and the earth, and actively seeks to bring this vision to realization."[12]

Thus, feminism in its most fundamental meaning represents a position, a belief, a perspective, and a movement that is opposed to discrimination based on gender. It is therefore opposed to sexism in all of its forms, whether within institutional structures and practices, attitudes and behaviors, or ideologies, beliefs, and theories that establish and reinforce gender discrimination. In terms of social structure, feminism is opposed to gendered patterns of domination and subordination, gendered role differentiation, gender-biased unequal access to goods and services. In addition, feminism is opposed to other forms of unjust discrimination and patterns of domination. It includes in its analysis the socially constructed connections among gender, race, class, age, sexual orientation, and other particular characterizations that can be the basis of discrimination and oppression.[13]

10. Spacks, *The Female Imagination*, 4–5.

11. Bhasin and Khan, Feminism in South Asia, 2–3. As cited in Bande & Atma, *Woman in Indian Short Stories*, 19.

12. Schneiders, *Beyond Patching*, 15.

13. Curran and Others, ed. *Feminist Ethics*, 5.

Patriarchy

At one level, patriarchy is understood as an ideology, which arose out of men's power to exchange women between kinship groups; as a symbolic male principle; as an expression of male control over women's sexuality and fertility; and to describe the institutional structure of male domination.[14] At another level, the concept of patriarchy is used to characterize the structures and social arrangements within which women's oppression is organized and maintained. Patriarchy is viewed as an institutionalized social practice diffused through all spheres of social life. Patriarchy not only extends to the family, but also to the control of the economy, polity, religion, medical science and many other institutions. This spread of patriarchal practice can be understood as "extended patriarchy."[15]

Thus, patriarchy in its narrow and traditional meaning refers to the system in which the male head of the household had absolute legal and economic power over his dependent female and male family members.[16] In its wider sense, it means the manifestation and institutionalization of male dominance over women and children in the family and the extension of male dominance over women in society in general. It implies that men hold power in all the important institutions of society and women have no access to such power. It does not imply that women are either totally powerless or deprived of their rights to impact society.

Gender

Gender represents not just the biological sex of an individual. It is not a synonym for sex. It is the cultural definition of behavior defined as appropriate to the sexes in a given society at a given time. Gender is a set of cultural roles. It refers to the widely shared expectations and norms within a society about appropriate male and female behavior, characteristics, and roles. It is a social and cultural construct that differentiates women from men, and defines the ways in which women and men interact with each other.

14. Rowbotham, "The Trouble with Patriarchy," 72–78.

15. Anjali writes that patriarchy involves "not simply the tracing of descent through the father . . . but any kind of group organization in which males hold dominant power and determine what part females shall or shall not play." Cf. Widge, "Patriarchy, Social Control and the Female Body," 39.

16. Patriarchy is defined by Letty M. Russel as the "rule of the father." It refers to systems of legal, social, economic, and political relations that validate and enforce the sovereignty of male heads of families over dependent persons in the household." For further detail see Russell & J. Shannon, eds. *Dictionary of Feminist Theologies*, 205.

Although sex-differentiated roles, rights, and obligations vary by class and life cycle stage, they exist in every sphere of human functioning (domestic, communal, labor market, religious, etc). This makes gender a fundamental dimension of societal stratification. These sex-specific roles, rights and obligations are not just different, but they also tend to be unequal. In almost every sphere of human functioning, the roles defined for women are fewer or less emancipating than those that men have. Unequal gender relations imply that men not only have and can exercise power greater than women in almost all spheres of functioning, but also have culturally and often legally sanctioned power over women and have greater control over them. This inequality in gender relations is embodied in various societal institutions, but is reproduced daily in the household.

SOCIOLOGICAL AND CULTURAL FACETS

The book treats the female body not in its anatomical, theological, or philosophical aspect, but in its sociological and cultural facets from an empirical perspective. This entails not merely a scrutiny of how the body is coded but also demands attention to the practices of women, which systematically constitute and animate the body. This would enable us to approach the body as women themselves see it rather than to restrict our attention to the idea of the body as 'given' or 'constructed.'

Besides, this book brings to light the perceptions of women with regard to their body and identifies *the changing status of the female body* today. Body has become increasingly central to the modern person's sense of self-identity. In today's context, the *agency* of female body assumes an importance, which has rarely been acknowledged or investigated either by sociologists[17] or by feminist anthropologists[18] and yet is central to our contemporary understanding of body in feminism.

17. Cf. Bourdieu, *Distinction: A Social Critique*; Bryan Turner, *Religion and Social Theory*; Idem, *The Body and Society*; Idem, *Regulating Bodies*; Goffman, *The Presentation of Self*; Douglas, Purity *and Danger*; Foucault, "Body/Power".

18. Initially, feminist anthropology focused on analysis and development of theory to explain the subordination of women, which seemed to be universal and cross-cultural. Anthropologists such as Rosaldo, Edholm, and Ortner used dichotomies such as public/domestic, production/reproduction, and nature/culture (respectively) to explain universal female subordination. In the late 1970's many feminist anthropologists were beginning to question the concept of universal female subordination and the usefulness of models based on dichotomies. Moreover the term gender which came to

Agency[19] implies that people have the ability to choose their goals and act (more or less rationally) to achieve them, as opposed to actions and ideas being determined by one's social position, genes, subconsciously impersonal historical forces, or other factors. In this book, *agency* is seen as an element of autonomy, which women exercise to take hold of their bodies. Hence, bringing to light this aspect of the female body is the core concern of this book.

RESEARCH DESIGN

Keeping in mind the objectives of the book, I have adopted the following research designs, namely exploratory, descriptive, analytical and interpretative, to bring to light the agency of Tamil women.

Exploratory Design

First of all, there is insufficient systematic information available about the differing perceptions of Tamil women with regard to their bodies. Therefore, the present book is purely exploratory. A detailed and in-depth exploratory analysis of the perceptions of Tamil women falls within the scope of the present book.

Descriptive and Analytical Designs

Secondly, the book is 'descriptive' and 'analytical' and is concerned about how women perceive their bodies through labor, marriage, sexuality, beauty, menstruation, space, and health. To better understand and analyze their perceptions with their background, the book describes the socio-cultural and geographical settings of the district of Dindigul, as

---

replace the term woman in the anthropological discussions, helped to free the issue of inequality from biological connotations. These new discussions of gender brought with them more complex issues of cross-cultural translation, universality, the relationship between thought systems and individual action, and also between ideology and material conditions. It has been intimately tied to the study of gender and its construction by various societies, an interest that examines both women and men. Cf. Mead, Sex and Temperament; Idem, Male and Female; Rosaldo, and Louise, eds., Women, Culture, and Society; Reiter, ed. Toward an Anthropology of Women; Ortner, Making Gender; Idem, "Is Female to Male as Nature is to Culture?," 402–13. Reprint in Anthropological Theory, eds. John McGee and Richard Worms (CA: Mayfield Publishing Company, 1974). And also Leonardo, *Gender at the Crossroads of Knowledge*; Levinson and Melvin, *Encyclopedia of Cultural Anthropology*, 519–24.

19. Anthropologists would treat *agency* as "the human capacity to act."

well as the variables like age, marital status, educational qualification, occupational and income status, type of family, use of media, involvement in movements or self-help groups, domicile and the caste background of the women respondents.

Interpretative Design

Thirdly, the book is 'interpretative' and concerned with identifying changes and elements of agency in women's perceptions of their bodies. As a micro level research, it goes into the intricacies of the daily lives of these women, into their world-views, values and perspectives. The book goes beyond viewing woman's body as a passive recipient of patriarchal conditionings. Rather it explores the dynamics of strategic options exercised by individual women. It also seeks to understand the impact of macro factors, which cause a change of perception.

METHOD OF INQUIRY

Being an inquiry into the socio-cultural perceptions of female body and the method of data collection being qualitative in its approach, I had placed this whole research within a feminist framework but adopting a combined methodology of phenomenology, grounded theory and feminist methodology.

The methodology of Phenomenology studies conscious experience from the subjective or first person point of view, analyzing the structure—types, intentional forms and meanings, dynamics, and (certain) enabling conditions—of perception, thought, imagination, emotion, and volition and action. Using this, I attempted to explore the relationship between states of individual consciousness and social life through the informant's eyes without being obstructed by pre-conceptions and theoretical notions. As a result, this enabled me to perceive things as they appear or the ways things are experienced.

In the case of grounded theory, it is most accurately described as a research method in which the theory is developed from the data, rather than the other way around. It moves from the specific to the more general. Besides, it is also a qualitative research method that uses a systematic set of procedures to develop an inductively derived grounded theory about a phenomenon.[20]

20. Glaser & Anselm, *The Discovery of Grounded Theory*; Cf. also Strauss, *Qualitative*

In order to maintain the "groundedness" of the approach among the women of Dindigul district, I consciously combined the data collection and analysis and used the initial data analysis to shape continuing data collection. This provided me with opportunities to increase the "density" and "saturation" of recurring categories, as well as to assist in providing follow-up procedures in regard to unanticipated results. Interlacing data collection and analysis in this manner also increased insights and clarified the parameters of the emerging theory. At the same time, this method supported the actions of initial data collection and preliminary analyses before attempting to incorporate previous research literature. This guarantees that my analysis is based on the data and that pre-existing constructs do not influence my analysis or the subsequent formation of the theory.

Feminist Research Methodology

In the case of feminist methodology, it is one set of approaches to the problems of producing justifiable knowledge of gender relations.[21] Although many feminist authors seem to draw upon certain elements as its defining features, there is no research technique that is distinctively feminist,[22] and there is no one method or strategy for feminist research, which is based on cultural and sociological context.[23]

Besides, feminist methodology also argues that research on women's experiences cannot be captured adequately through quantitative methods. On the contrary, qualitative methods allow us to know people personally and to see them as they develop their own definitions of the world. We experience what they experience in their daily struggles in their society. We learn about groups and experiences about which we

---

Analysis for Social Scientists; Strauss and Juliet, *Basics of Qualitative Research: Grounded Theory Procedures and Techniques.*

21. Ramazanoglu and Janet, *Feminist Methodology*, 10; also Eisenstein, *Contemporary Feminist Thought*; Hermann, and Abigail, eds., *Theorizing Feminism*; Jackson, and Jackie, eds., *Contemporary Feminist Theories*; Moi, *Sexual/ Textual Politics*; Morgen, ed. *Gender and Anthropology.*

22. Ramazanoglu and Janet, *Feminist Methodology*, 15. Cf. also Agarwala, *Directory of Women's Studies in India.*

23. Richardson and Victoria, *Introduction to Women Studies.*

may have known nothing.[24] It has the aim of understanding experiences as closely as possible and as its participants feel or live it.[25]

In the search for a relevant methodology, I had used a qualitative data research style to recapitulate the lived experiences of women, to bring about feminist consciousness,[26] and to allow women to speak for themselves on their perspectives.

Therefore, what makes this research feminist are the motives, concerns and knowledge brought to the research process. I have emphasized women's experiences as the primary source for theorizing, and have used narratives to translate their experiences from real life into a text.

DESCRIPTION OF TOOLS

The following few commonly used qualitative tools were employed in the process of data collection.

* Participant Observation
* Face to face unstructured in-depth interviews
* Focused Group Discussions
* Distribution of a Questionnaire

Participant Observation

Bernard Russel makes it clear that, through participant observation one establishes rapport in a new community; learning to act so that people go about their business as usual when you show up; and removing yourself everyday from cultural immersion so that you can intellectualize what you've learned, put it into perspective, and write about it convincingly.[27] Hence the author adopted participant observation as the first tool for the study in order to get close to women and make them feel comfortable enough with the author's presence, so that the author could closely ob-

24. Periannan, *Social Research Methodology*, 133; also cf. Young, *Scientific Social Survey*.

25. Russel, *Research Methods in Anthropology*.

26. During the process of data collection, many respondents were conscientised and brought to awareness of their real situation. Gokilvani, "Feminist Research Methodology," 104–5. Cf. Also Stanley and Sue, *Breaking out Feminist Consciousness*, 54–59.

27. Russel, *Research Methods in Anthropology*.

serve and record information about their perceptions concerning their bodies. The author spent almost twelve months in the field immersing herself in the setting, observing and being a participant in the process of the research.

Face to Face Unstructured In-depth Interviews

Face to face unstructured in-depth interview method was used to elicit from women their perceptions on their own bodies. The primary intent of these interviews was to journey with these women by listening to their stories of agony, anguish and ecstasy, and to discover attentively their self-perception of the body. Further, the method facilitated supplementary data-collection through observation during visits to the places and crosschecking of the responses for ensuring their reliability. For gathering a wide range of personal data from the illiterate respondents, interview was the only option.

The interview schedule was divided into three parts. The first part consisted of items relating to the socio-economic background of the respondents such as caste, religion, education, occupation, economic status, and other details. The second part contained specific questions intended to elicit their perceptions about their body. The third part was the most important as it included questions on chastity, marriage, space, beauty, health, labor and motherhood. As a matter of fact, the analysis of data collected in this third part constitutes the substantive part of this study. Almost 100 women were interviewed in depth. To check the reliability and validity of the interview schedule, it was pre-tested on 15 women. The final schedule was prepared after making necessary modifications as warranted by the pre-test.

Focused Group Discussions

Apart from the interview schedule, I also held 15 focused group discussions with the women respondents. Focus groups consisted of 7 to 10 people. These discussions fostered interaction, openness and freedom to articulate their opinions in some depth among women respondents. It also helped as many respondents as possible to participate in the discussions. Besides, these discussions enabled me, who am an outsider, to understand and describe better the range of perspectives of the participants with regard to their bodies.

Distribution of the Questionnaire

The last part of the schedule was the distribution of a questionnaire with simple and clear questions directly related to women's body, intended mainly to make as many women as possible to participate. It was prepared and used to obtain the data from the women respondents selected for the study. After the questionnaire was formulated, a pilot study was made among twenty-five women. A few questions, which posed problems of comprehension and were unclear to the respondents, were modified in the final questionnaire.

I distributed the questionnaire to 500 women respondents. This provided opportunity to the respondents to express their views concerning the issue under study. The questions were directly related to motherhood, marriage, menstruation, beauty, space, labor and health. The format of the questionnaire is attached in Appendix I.

Rapport Building

Being a woman from the Tamil soil, belonging to the same culture and language, and having an experience in working for the cause of other women, it was easy for me to build a rapport with women respondents. The respondents felt at home with me during the focused group discussions, filling up of the questionnaire, and also during the in-depth interviews. The respondents were always contacted in their homes. In the case of educated women respondents, they themselves filled up the questionnaire, whereas in the case of illiterate women, their answers were filled up by the field workers of the Self Help Groups (SHG), or by other educated women but this was always done in their presence.

All the same, the spell of fieldwork was not entirely smooth, as the investigator had to face many hurdles in getting sufficient time with the respondents during their busy schedule. Moreover, the locale of the study being spread over a wide area caused additional problems in the work of investigation. The interviews and focused group discussions were not held at times and places that suited the respondents. The redeeming point was that all the respondents were involved and interested in the objective of the study. Some of the respondents took special interest in the questionnaire and gave information about their experiences by inviting the author to their homes. Some of them were frank and fearless in expressing their views, which in turn helped the author to understand their viewpoint in depth; while others appeared to be rather hesitant in discussing issues like body and sexuality.

Delimitations of the Study

First of all, due to the vastness of the subject, this research has necessarily to limit itself to women's perception of their body with regard to menstruation, marriage, sexuality, beauty, labor and space. It does not attempt to make a study of other areas such as the media, fine arts, pornography, health, etc.

Secondly, since there was no previous survey made on the area of female body, this study did not have precedents to go by. Therefore, the study, as has already been mentioned, is of an exploratory and descriptive nature.

Thirdly, the study limits itself to the self-perceptions of *married women* with regard to their body. Other details like the society's view and the men's view on women's body were not the concern of this study.

Fourthly, as a feminist and a woman from Tamilnadu, it was not difficult to understand the range of ideologies that women had with regard to their bodies. In this sense, I was an *insider* to the community and had the advantage of knowing and being able to take for granted certain aspects of Tamil women's perceptions. However, there were other considerations such as my civil and religious (single and belonging to a Roman Catholic religious order) status that contributed to an *outsider* position in the community. While as an *insider*, I could share some of the experiences of the respondents, as an *outsider* I strove to observe and listen to their experiences.

Finally, I have not been able to disclose the names of the respondents in the research for obvious reasons.

Analysis and Interpretation of Data

The analysis is based on the data collected from the field through various tools. The purpose of analysis is to summarize the completed observations in such a manner that they yield answers to the research questions. It is the purpose of interpretation to search for the broader meaning of the answers by linking them to other available knowledge. I adopted mainly content analysis in order to investigate the thematic content of the communication and to make inferences from it.

CONCEPTUAL FRAMEWORK

Today the question of *human agency* is central to all discussions in the social field. The idea of men and women as acting subjects is much discussed in contemporary social science discourse. This research engages in exploring how, amidst the patriarchal conditionings, women actively negotiate and exercise their *agency* to take control of their bodies. The author uses *agency* as a conceptual framework for the analysis and interpretation of the field data on the socio-cultural perceptions of the female body by the women of Dindigul district. She does not, however, suggest that all women of Dindigul District experience total bodily freedom to be what they are and to do what they want. While oppression of women still plays an important role and their body is increasingly confined to a certain space, a small group of women do reconstruct their identity. Hence, my focus on *agency* is not a denial of the cruel realities vis-à-vis female bodies.

Drawing inspiration from Erving Goffman, a sociologist, and Seemanthini Niranjana, a feminist cultural anthropologist, the research positions itself within the conceptual framework of *agency*, especially on how women exercise *agency* to take control of their bodies.

The book also incorporates some of the important notions on *empowerment as agency* as viewed and proposed by Sunita Kishor and Kamala Gupta in their paper on "Women's Empowerment in India and Its States: Evidence from the NFHS."[28] Although with regard to my stand about *agency* I advocate the claims of the above paper, nonetheless, I do not limit my view of *agency* to these authors alone, but have attempted to go beyond them and have worked out my own notion of *agency*.

Erving Goffman's Standpoint of Body as Agency[29]

In sociology, the body, both in its material aspects and social relatedness, was not researched seriously until the work of Erving Goffman. In comparison with Foucault, who focuses on how the body is invested with powers that control individuals, Erving Goffman's writings appear to-

28. Cf. Kishor and Kamala, "Women's Empowerment in India," 694–712.

29. Erving Goffman has authored the following books and articles: *Behavior in Public Places*; Idem, *Stigma: Notes on the Management of Spoiled Identity*; Idem, *The Presentation of Self*; Idem, *Frame Analysis*; Idem, "The Arrangement between the Sexes," 301–31; Idem, Gender Advertisement; Idem, "The interaction order,"; Idem, "The arrangement between the sexes."

place more emphasis on the body as integral to human *agency.* Goffman says, "The body enables people to intervene in, and make a difference to the flow of daily life."[30] However, embodied individuals are not autonomous in Goffman's work. His analysis of the `shared vocabularies of body idiom' (or conventional forms of non-verbal language), which guide people's perceptions of bodily appearances and performances, provides a sense of the social constraints under which body management occurs. For Goffman, the body is important for identifying the links between people's self and social identities.[31]

There are three main features that characterize Goffman's approach to the body.

First, he views the body "as the material property of individuals."[32] In contrast to naturalistic views, which portray people's actions and identities as determined by their biological bodies, Goffman argues, "individuals usually have the ability to control and monitor their bodily performances in order to facilitate social interaction."[33] Here, the body is associated with the exercise of human agency, and it appears in Goffman's work as a resource, which both requires and enables people to manage their movements and appearances.

Secondly, he is of the opinion that "the body is not actually produced by social forces,"[34] as in Foucault's work. According to Goffman the meanings attributed to the body are determined by `shared vocabularies of body idiom,' which are not under the immediate control of individuals.[35] Body idiom is a conventionalized form of non-verbal communication, which is by far the most important component of behavior in public. It is used by Goffman in a general sense to refer to dress, bearing, movements and position, sound level, physical gestures such as waving or saluting, facial decorations, and broad emotional expressions.[36] This is what he calls 'techniques of the body in social relationships.'[37] This also allows one to classify information signaled by bodies and shared

30. Goffman, *The Presentation of Self*, 34.

31. Goffman, *The Presentation of Self*; Idem, *Gender Advertisement*.

32. Goffman, *The Presentation of Self*, 56.

33. Ibid., 62.

34. Ibid., 71.

35. Goffman, *Behavior in Public Places*, 35.

36. Ibid., 33.

37. Goffman, *The Presentation of Self*, 82.

vocabularies of body idiom. It provides categories which label and grade people hierarchically according to this information. Consequently, these classifications exert a profound influence on the ways in which individuals seek to manage and present their bodies.

These first two features of Goffman's approach suggest that human bodies have a dual location. Bodies are the property of individuals, yet are defined as significant and meaningful by society. This formulation lies at the core of the third main feature of Goffman's approach to the body.

Third, Goffman also views the role played by the body "in mediating the relationship between people's self-identity and their social identity."[38] The social tends to become internalized and exert a powerful influence on an individual's sense of self and feelings of inner worth. For instance, self-care regimes are not simply about preventing disease; they are also concerned with making us feel good about how our bodies appear to others and ourselves. Health has become increasingly associated with appearance and what Goffman has termed the 'presentation of self.'[39] Thus in nutshell, according to Goffman, the human body has the elements of *agency* inherent in it, to intervene and to make a difference in the daily flow of life.

Seemanthini Niranjana's View of Agency[40]

Within the theoretical framework of *space,* Niranjana treats *agency* as that which, delineates space into public and private, with the former being described as an overtly political domain as, in fact, the domain of power.[41] The relative marginalization of women from this domain, consequently, gets interpreted as a sign of their powerlessness and lack of *agency.*[42] However, her focus on power is 'less as a unitary, monolithic structure and more as a sort of tenuous space, constantly fractured by the contestatory acts and gestures of subordinates.'[43]

38. Ibid., 87.

39. Ibid.

40. Seemanthini Niranjana is an Indian feminist anthropologist. She has authored the following articles and book. "Discerning Women," 393–412; Idem, "On Gender and Difference," 28–41; Idem, "Femininity, Space and the Female Body," 107–24.

41. Niranjana, *Gender and Space*, 88.

42. Ibid., 88.

43. Ibid.

Quoting Foucault's definition of power, she draws an insight for her own understanding of *agency*.

[P]ower . . . is not that which makes the difference between those who exclusively possess and retain it and those who do not have it and submit to it. Power must be analyzed as something, which circulates . . . (Individuals), are not only inert or consenting targets; they are always also the elements of its articulation.[44]

Drawing upon this insight, Niranjana attempts a further inflection into the edifice of *agency* and women. Seemingly, she understands *agency* in relation to women's lives as that which has often taken the form of resistance offered against the exercise of power. She attempts to read resistance into women's acts within the so-called private sphere itself,[45] and defines women's *agency* in terms of a 'transformative capacity,' meaningful only within a 'politics of change.'[46]

An Interpretative Framework on Agency: Perspectives and Clarifications

In keeping with recent trends in contemporary social theory, I have tried to make conceptual room for the notion that, humans, both as individuals and organized collectivities are knowledgeable and skilled actors who make choices and thereby go about constructing the social world in which they live. When we look at our own lives, we have a sense that we are answerable for many of the things that have happened to us, and are in some sense responsible for some of the things that have happened to those around us.

Irrespective of their cultural or historical location, humans are seen as having a psychological need for meaning, which compels them to act.[47] Giddens's analysis of ontological security implies that humans have a fundamental and unchanging need to feel secure about the basic parameters of themselves and the world around them. Therefore, every animate body has an innate element of agency in it.[48] Chris Shilling says,

44. M. Foucault, "Body/Power," 98.

45. Hanlon, "Issues of Widowhood," 62–108; Raheja and Gold, *Listen to the Heron's Words*.

46. Niranjana, *Gender and Space*, 88.

47. Abercrombie, "Knowledge, order and human anatomy."

48. Humans are not simply objects affected by external forces; humans are also subjects who exercise *agency*. They have power to affect their environment in a conscious

"A body is an integral component of human agency."[49] It is our bodies, which allow us to act, to intervene in and to alter the flow of daily life. Indeed, it is impossible to have an adequate theory of human agency without taking into account the body. In a very important sense, acting people are acting bodies.[50] In view of the above discussion, my understanding of *agency* in relation to women entails the important characteristic of *empowerment*, as manifested in assertion, critical consciousness, resistance and autonomy within the respective structures.

Empowerment as Apparent Indication of Agency

At this point, it is necessary to be explicit about what we mean by the term 'empowerment.' While several authors have tried to capture the meaning of the word, the definition most relevant to the approach taken in this research is the one provided by Sen and Batliwala:[51]

> Empowerment is the process by which the powerless gain greater control over the circumstances of their lives. It includes both control over resources and over ideology . . . (includes, in addition to extrinsic control) a growing intrinsic capability—greater self-confidence, and an inner transformation of one's consciousness that enables one to overcome external barriers . . .

Inherent in this definition are two important ideas, the first of which is that empowerment is not about power over others (a feature of domination), but *power to achieve goals and ends*. By conceptualizing empowerment in terms of 'power to' the definition explicitly recognizes that the process of empowerment involves not only changes in access to resources, but also an understanding of one's rights and entitlements and the conscientization that 'gender roles can be changed and gender equality is possible.'

The second important idea is that the concept of empowerment is more generally applicable to those who are powerless, whether male or female individuals or a group, class or caste. Hence, there is nothing about the concept of empowerment *per se* which applies to women alone. Nonetheless, women's empowerment or lack of it, is unique in that it cuts

---

and intentional way. Cf. Giddens, *The Constitution of Society*, 14–16.

49. Shilling, *The Body*, 9.

50. Ibid.

51. As cited in Malhotra et al., "Measuring Women's Empowerment."

across all types of class and caste powerlessness and unlike class or caste powerlessness, is played out also within families and households.[52]

While empowerment literally means 'to invest with power,' in the context of women's empowerment, the term has come to denote that a woman has increased control over her own life, body, and environment. In discussions of women's empowerment, emphasis is often placed on women's decision-making roles, their economic self-reliance, and their legal rights to equal treatment, inheritance and protection against all forms of discrimination in addition to the elimination of barriers to their access to resources such as education and information. [53]

Sunita Kishor's three-pronged approach describing the level of women's *empowerment* will help us further in understanding the term. She argues that capturing the empowerment process with cross-sectional data needs not only indicators that evaluate the end-product of the process (i.e., indicators that measure evidence of empowerment), but also indicators of women's access to different sources of empowerment and of women's location within an appropriate setting for empowerment. Such measures would include women's participation in household decision-making, financial autonomy and freedom of movement, as well as measures that suggest a rejection of the gender-based subordination of women.

Potential sources of empowerment are those that provide the building blocks of empowerment: knowledge and potential advantage in the access to and control of resources. These indicators cannot be considered evidence of empowerment because there is no guarantee that the powerless will use, or will be in a position to use, these tools to become empowered. Nonetheless, access to resources remains an intrinsic component of empowerment. Indicators of the setting or conditions for empowerment refer to the circumstances of the respondent's current and past environment: factors that are likely to condition the outlook

52. Ibid. The same view is also shared by Giddens in his definition on agency and power. Agency implies power. Agency concerns events of which an individual is the perpetrator, in the sense that the individual could, at any phase in a given sequence of conduct, have acted otherwise. If an individual intervenes at the right time, she/he becomes an agent. An agent is . . . able to deploy, in the flow of daily life, a range of casual powers, including that of influencing those deployed by others. Cf. Giddens, *The Constitution*, 9 & 14.

53. Germaine and Rachel, *The Cairo Consciousness*; United Nations (1995): *Population and Development*.

and opportunities available to the respondent. These can include, for example, indicators of current and past living arrangements and characteristics of people who directly influence the opportunities available to the respondent.

Thus, empowerment can be defined as the means by which individuals, groups and communities are able to take control of their circumstances and achieve their own goals, thereby being able to work towards helping themselves and others to maximize the quality of their lives.

Assertion as Agency

Assertion is to state an opinion or claim a right or to establish authority forcefully. A woman, for example, who is assertive, behaves confidently and is not afraid to say what she wants or believes in. If a woman is able to think for herself and articulate her needs and wants, then she has agency. This also implies communicating anything confidently and obtaining what one wants.

Autonomy as Agency

Autonomy implies freedom from oppressive restrictions. In the case of women, it is freedom from biological and societal restrictions. Autonomy is self-determination which means being free to decide one's own destiny; being free to define one's social role and space; having the freedom to make decisions concerning one's body. Autonomy means earning one's own status, not being born into it or marrying it; it means financial independence; freedom to choose one's lifestyle and sexual preference—all of which implies a radical transformation of existing institutions, values and theories. If a woman has autonomy to decide for herself and do what she wants, then there is agency embedded in her action. Scholars contend that one of the major objectives of women's liberation movements has been to free women from the cultural demand for self-effacement and to establish their right to full human development.[54]

Critical Consciousness as Agency

A woman can be said to possess *agency* if she has critical consciousness of all that she hears, sees and does and has a capacity to critique the age-

54. Paris, *Imagined Human Beings*, 39.

old perceptions regarding her body—motherhood, pregnancy, beauty, space, etc. The ability to raise questions is an indicator of agency.

To conclude, The five statements given below more or less clarify the concept of *agency* used in the present research.

For a woman *agency* means

1. Having a sense of autonomy and self-confidence in managing her own life.
2. Having freedom to use her bodily abilities to the fullest for her well-being as well as that of society.
3. Having adequate power and status to fight against all deprivations, abuse and discrimination.
4. Being independent, particularly in economic matters, and having authority in decision-making in the family and in personal life.
5. Daring to deconstruct and decode myths and notions that keep her under control so that they do not influence her life adversely.

Thus *agency* for women is in breaking their silence, asserting their individualities and recognizing their bodily needs and sexual drives, and moving "beyond the region of blind contentment"[55] to defy the conventional sanctions.

Conclusion

Having clarified the concepts, methodology and theoretical framework in the book, we now move on to explore the socio-cultural perceptions of the women respondents with regard to their bodies.

55. Chopin, *The Awakening*, 74.

3

Socio-Cultural Perceptions of the Female Body

THIS CHAPTER ATTEMPTS TO explore in depth, the socio-cultural perceptions of women from Dindigul district, Tamilnadu, India with regard to their bodies. As already mentioned in the second chapter, this book is purely empirical, and it follows in the main a qualitative method. A stratified random and purposive sampling was done, ensuring however a representation of women of all religions (Hindus, Muslim and Christians), of BCs, MBCs and Dalits, of literates and illiterates, of the employed and the unemployed, of rural and urban, of those who view the media and those who never view the media and of those who are involved in action-oriented groups and those who are not. The data collected through participant observation, in-depth unstructured interviews and focused group discussions among one hundred and fifty women spread over seven taluks of Dindigul district, are analyzed in the light of grounded theory. The data were coded, categorized, and grouped together to find certain patterns.

As it was already said, the data and the findings shown in this chapter are texts culled out from the responses of the qualitative interviews. Besides, in the process of the analysis of the data, the author has highlighted in the text *only* those striking differences that are seen among the variables. Moreover, in all these voices of women, identifying the elements of *agency* is the prime concern and the main focus of this book. They help us to understand the changing trend among women in Tamilnadu, especially with regard to the perceptions of their bodies. The book also focuses on the factors, which might have led them to exercise agency.

The various themes that are covered in these pages are space, motherhood, menstruation, beauty, kaṟpu, sexuality, and labor, and labor. I delineate the various factors in women's perceptions of their bodies.

They are the perceptions of the respondents, the underlying attitudes of these perceptions, the elements of agency in the perceptions and the supportive factors of the respondents.

What the respondents said was edited for grammar, but the sentence structure is preserved as far as possible, so as to disclose, as far as possible, their feelings, hesitations, courage and so on.

For statistical count, the author has used simple counts. They indicate only the density of categories present in the qualitative data. Such counts are mentioned in the text itself to indicate the frequency of a category.

This chapter is organized in line with the first three objectives of this book.

1. To explore the differing socio-cultural perceptions of women with regard to their bodies.
2. To study the exercise of women's *agency* in the perceptions of their bodies.
3. To inquire into the major factors leading to differing perceptions among women regarding their bodies.

The perceptions of women with regard to their bodies at different phases of their life-cycle as shared by the respondents as well as observed by me are classified and presented here under appropriate titles.

BODY AND SPACE

One of the perceptions that surround a woman's body concerns space. Space refers to that which allows a person to move, maneuver, and negotiate to develop one's capabilities.

Space: Right inside

Recognition of the household as women's space is widely prevalent among the women respondents.[1] Most often, the kind of spaces that women inhabit are related to the domestic work they do. The kitchen is considered primarily their space. In many households of the extended

1. The divide between the 'male' public space and 'female' private space is seen as one of the most oppressive aspects of women's lives.

type, women are disallowed into certain other areas of the house.[2] It was evident that most of the respondents in the course of their household chores rarely venture beyond certain conventional boundaries. This was also seen mostly in their movements in and around the fence / compound of their house and in their attitude towards work outside.

Ponmalar[3] for instance said, "Usually I go to temple or to the tap to collect water. What else a woman needs? A good husband who provides all that she needs, viz., a house, children, and money to buy one's daily needs and wants. It is good that a woman remains inside the house, so that unnecessary problems can be avoided." Such a perception was not only that of Ponmalar but also of the 54 percent of the women respondents[4] whom I interviewed. This indicates that it is only in the space inside and around the house, together with areas associated with domestic labor—the wells, taps, the neighbors' fence and places of worship—which the women seemed to be comfortable with themselves, because they consider these places as unproblematic and not in need of legitimation.

Kokila 40, a housewife said, "As long as Sita[5] remained within the Lakṣmaṇa-rēka[6] she was safe." This brings home the myth of Sita, which reminds the women of their restricted space. They frequently used proverbs that stress women's space as *inside*. To cite an example, peṇṇukku vīṭu tāṉ ulakam: āṇukku ulakamē vīṭu meaning 'For a woman, home is her world; whereas for a man, the world is his home.'

Thus, the association between women and the domestic sphere structures women's bodily access to space. Although such an attitude towards woman's space was found in all categories of the respondents,

2. In their books, Deshmukh and Niranjana discuss about the issue of how women are forbidden to enter certain areas. Cf. Deshmukh—Ranadive, *Space for Power*, 61; Niranjana, *Gender and Space*, 49.

3. This text and all the other texts within the quotation marks are the reports of conversation with women respondents of Dindigul District unless otherwise indicated.

4. Among the 150 total respondents, 54 percent of them consider their space as right inside their homes.

5. Sita is a heroine of one of the great Indian epics called *Ramayana*.

6. Lakṣmaṇa-rēka: This event takes place in the Indian great epic called *Ramayana*. When Rama, the hero of the epic left for forest, he left his wife Sita under his brother Laksmana's care. Laksmana, the brother of Rama is supposed to have drawn a line before he left Sita alone. Sita was told not to cross the line under any circumstances. The Lakṣmaṇa-rēka is rich with symbolic overtones. It is also a form of constraint, a line, which Sita, as woman had no right to cross over. It was a boundary drawn by a male, who had been deputed by another male to guard Sita, the female.

yet there was a significant difference between respondents who are employed outside and those unemployed, namely, the housewives.

Parvati 40, a housewife said, "Women are supposed to stay inside the homes as much as possible. When women are seen on the roadside, the society speaks ill of them. That's why we prefer to remain inside. When people speak ill of us, it is a shame for our family too. In order to preserve our kuṭumpa kauravam (family prestige) and name, we prefer to stay inside our homes." A sense of shame and preoccupation for kuṭumpa kauravam were the main reasons found among these respondents. The data manifests that among the housewives,[7] 64 percent consider their space as right *inside* their homes while in the case of those employed it was only 23 percent.

Analysis of the data indicates that women who are employed outside have a broader understanding of space than the housewives. This probably may be due to the situations of housewives who have limited exposure to the outside world. This confirms the author's observation that the women unexposed to the outside world tend to hold on to a conventional ideology of the body as normative and confine themselves to the fixed boundaries.[8] Moreover, 55 percent of these housewives are solely dependent on their husbands for their survival. Most likely this also may be another reason for these women to hold onto the traditions regarding their space.

In the same way, there was a significant difference among women of different religion with regard to the perception of woman's space. Only 27 percent Christian and 38 percent Hindu women said that the woman's space is right inside their homes, while in the case of Muslim women, it was 78 percent. To cite an example, Kaajimujja 45, a Muslim said, "Women are instructed in our religion not to go out and roam around on the streets. So we avoid going out. If we disobey, we will be punished by our men."

The influence of religious teaching on Muslim women is clearly seen in the analysis of the data. It makes them believe that their space is right inside their homes, thus depriving them autonomy even to go where they want. Moreover, among the Muslim respondents, 66 percent of them are homebound. Therefore, this is also another reason for them to consider their space as right inside their homes.

7. Among the total respondents, 41 percent are housewives. They remain at home, taking care of the family affairs.

8. G. Vijayeswari Rao also observes this in her book, *Women and Society*, 71.

Women, Work, and Space

Although women are to carry out the responsibility of looking after the household affairs, yet they should be in the vicinity of their family members. The respondents are of the opinion that as much as possible women must work close to their homes. Eswari 39, a housewife said, "It is good that women go to earn to manage the family expenses. But as much as possible a woman must work close to her house or village, so that she can get back home soon."

The respondents who work in organized sectors are encouraged to work in the same or close-by village or town, and certainly not far away.[9] In the case of unorganized work, women mostly work in the or in the tōṭṭam (farm), which is either in the village or in the nearby villages. Only flowers, fruits and vegetable vendors and those who are involved in construction work, move into close-by cities and towns. Women who go for work are found returning home without delay. They assume that if they return immediately a lot of problem will disappear from the family.

In an unstructured interview Manjula 38, a clerk in the Government office, said,

"As soon as my work in the office is over, I get back home. Because if I come late, my husband questions me and makes me feel embarrassed. Sometimes he even doubts me. So I prefer to remain within the house. Otherwise, I will be labeled with all sorts of titles like aṭaṅkāppiṭāri, ōṭukāli (a loose woman) etc., and my family morality will be affected too."

Such sharing underscores women's internalisation of patriarchal spatial strategies, which determine women's space as right inside their homes, and guarantees of their bodily safety and moral reputation even when they go for work outside.

Bodily Mobility and Male Company

The perception of body space is also seen in women's attitude in going out alone or going out in the nights without company, preferably male company. In the course of their daily life and activities, women negotiate a variety of situations and circumstances that take them beyond the physical space of the household. Starting with their typical household

9. I came across only six women respondents who said that they had sent their daughters to work in far-off places. The rest of them work in nearby towns or villages.

activities, namely the regular tasks of fetching water, collecting firewood, or tending the sheep or cows, women in rural areas go together or go in small groups or with someone, for fear of being attacked by a known or unknown person or by evil spirits. They believe that some spirits move around at night and some during the day. These spirits are popularly known as kāttu kāṟuppu. They are the spirits of those who committed suicide, or who have been murdered, or those who have died with unfulfilled desires. It is also believed that the spirits, which come during the day, move around in the forest areas or fields or in any lonely place, whereas the spirits, which visit at nights, move around in the residential areas, looking for a lone being, preferably women and children.

While describing a woman's space, Shameera Begum, 40, a housewife and a mother of four children said:

> If a woman wants her body to be safe then it is good that she remains where she is expected to be. I very rarely go out. Whether during the day or night, when I want to go out, I wait for my husband or for my 10 year old son to come home to take me out. Without them, I never go out. I visit my neighbors sometimes whose houses are very close. My husband does not like me going out and when he comes to know he gets angry and shouts at me. So I do not go out at all. And if I often go out, people also speak ill of my character.

In a focused group discussion, some of the respondents said that they always go with someone or together when they go to work in the field or to pluck flowers in the garden. They also believe that even a trip outside the house at night to urinate may bring on a demon attack on a woman's body, especially when it is menstruating. Therefore, women in menstruation, pregnancy, and child-birth are discouraged to go out alone at night. When they go out, they carry with them pieces of iron or neem leaves,[10] which they believe, will guard and protect their body from demons.[11]

10. Neem leaves symbolize the presence of the Hindu goddess, *Mari Amman*. In addition, people in India make use of these leaves to cast away the evil spirits.

11. During menstruation, certain communities isolate women completely or put them only in the company of other women. People think that menstrual blood is "unclean" and it gives menstruating women supernatural powers, which is sometimes good but more often destructive. Cf. also The Boston Women's Health Book Collective, *The NEW Our Bodies*, 212.

As much as possible, at night, women go out along with their family members, or relatives living close by. Even when they go to a petty shop to purchase something, they take someone with them to indicate that someone is aware of their whereabouts and to prove their moral credibility.[12] Women are afraid to go out alone at night mostly because of the fear of their name being spoilt than the mere danger of evil or the presence of other men.

For instance, in an unstructured interview Sundari, a nurse said, "I am afraid even to go out alone during the day. Then how will I go alone at night? I am afraid to look at men on the road. I have also a fear whether I would be attacked by a *by a* muṉi[13] if I go alone at night. So, I always go in the company of someone."

The song of Antoniammal, an elderly woman, substantiates this. She recited from her memory, an old Tamil folk song[14] which is chanted on the day of pūppuṉita nīrāṭṭu viḻā.

> Your breasts are maturing
> Your sharp teeth shine
> Your hair is in a top-knot
> You wear a cool leaf-dress.
> From now on
> Do not go here and there with your wandering girlfriends.
> Our ancient town has old places with attacking deities
> We are entrusted with the duty of protecting you.
> Do not go where you went before.
> You are no longer a little girl, O Wise child,
> But have become a woman.
> Do not go outside.

This brings to light how female puberty rites and ritual celebration lead the girl to a more confined territory. Besides, women's bodily movements are not only well-defined but they are also warned against men who could endanger their bodily safety.

12. While referring to body and space, Niranjana says that the spatial axis is not only deeply embedded in perceptual schemes but also decides bodily practices, as proper and improper, moral and immoral, and so on. Cf. Niranjana, "Femininity, Space," 16.

13. Muṉi is the spirit of the dead person.

14. She said that in olden days this folk song was sung at the time of pūppuṉita nīrāṭṭu viḻā to instruct the pubescent girls to discipline their body movements.

Such a perception illustrates women's internalization of the patriarchal mindset regarding women's bodies as weak[15] which can be attacked by a demon or by a man,[16] and men as potential rapists or threats to their bodily safety. The concept of morality is also at the rear of their minds, which control women's movements, especially after dusk. This points to how women's bodily movements are choreographed by certain implicit cultural rules, depriving them of autonomy to move beyond fixed boundaries.

Private Space vs. Public Space

Amidst the residual voices that co-exist with the ideas of the *inside* as an inviolable space for women, there are women who do not consider their space as right *inside* their home. Rather they dare to move out into society at anytime. A significant variation is seen among the respondents' geographical location, occupation and age group.

For instance, Radhika 42, a teacher, said:

> As long as I remained in my village I thought women should not go out except for serious reasons. I was afraid to go out also. But after I moved out into the city, my view of life has changed. It is only in the village people keep watching others. Here I move out freely. Moreover, in the cities, the life of a woman is different. She has to move out of her home if she wants to survive. If she remains inside, she will be ignorant of many things. The more she moves out, the broader her life turns out to be.

82 percent of the respondents who live either in semi-urban or urban setting were of this opinion.[17] Some of them even said that they feel completely free to move out at anytime. Thus it is apparent from the analysis of the data that the place of residence has an impact on women with regard to their understanding of space. In rural setting, women

15. The ideas of women as vulnerable, weak and in need of protection have a long history. Cf. Henning, "Don't Touch Me," 17. As a result there is an insistence on the part of the female body that needs to be protected by a stronger body which is male body. Cf. Wadley ed., *The Powers Of Tamil Women*, 77. This has kept the female body for long, in a weaker and timid position.

16. They did not encourage even me to visit their villages during the night. I was asked to come during the day. They saw to it that I left their villages before 7 pm. In case of delay in the work, two men from their village accompanied me to the bus stop.

17. In the case of rural women, it was only 32 percent who think differently regarding their space.

hesitate to go out alone, especially at night because of the fear of being watched closely. But urban life places women in a better position to move around freely (without the fear of being watched) and expand their bodily space.

Besides domicile, a remarkable difference is seen among women who are employed and those who remain at home as housewives (unemployed outside). Among the total respondents, 71 percent of the respondents who work outside[18] are of the opinion that going out for work has enabled them to understand better and expand their body space.

To cite an example, Meenaski said, "When I remained a housewife I used to suspect women who go for work. But after marriage, I had to go for work. In the beginning I was hesitant and worried. But slowly I have got rid of my fear. Today, I can go out alone, not only during the day but also during the nights. Moreover, my understanding of woman's space has also changed. Working outside has given me opportunities to see other women who risk their lives too."

Analysis of the above data brings to light that access to a place of work outside the house, agricultural / non-agricultural, has become a tool of empowerment. This enables them not only to deconstruct the space set by patriarchal society but also to re-map their own space.

However, it is apparent that when it is a matter of *venturing into new space* women in unorganized sectors are more daring than those in organized sectors. The words of Manjula[19] confirmed this. Though employed in the organized sector, still she finds herself loaded with the traditional understanding of woman's space as right *inside*.

Besides, those employed in unorganized sectors had different reasons for their understanding of space.

For instance Devi, an unorganized laborer, asked, "Who will feed my children when they cry for food? My husband is a drunkard and what he earns goes for his drinking. How can I sit at home? So I go for work. Sometimes I go and work in other villages and do ploughing and wood-cutting[20] also. Because of that, people speak ill of me, and they doubt my character. But I am least bothered about what they say."

18. During my visit, I observed that some of the respondents were employed in their house itself. They were mostly employed in rolling beedis, stringing flowers, garlands, etc.

19. See the statement of Manjula above under the title 'Women, Work, and Space.'

20. Men usually carry out Ploughing and woodcutting.

Such assertions were not only from Devi but also from 72 percent of the respondents who work in unorganized sectors. This is because of the condition of unorganized laborers. They are mostly responsible for the household affairs. If they do not go out, they cannot survive. According to the data, 83 percent of the unorganized laborers were responsible for their household affairs. In order to meet their daily survival needs, they take any risks, which is not the case with those who work in organized sectors.

What emerges from this is whether in the organized sector or the unorganized sector, in the case of women shouldering fully the family responsibility, there is no difference between private space and public space. Thus it can be inferred that, when the concern is survival, women move from the private to the public space breaking the patriarchal norms which demarcate their body and space.

BODILY Aṭakkam[21]

Another pre-dominant perception that is very prevalent among the respondents of the Dindigul district is restraint of the body. A woman's body has to be modest, docile and self-restrained always. Though the disciplining of the female body starts right at the beginning of childhood, it gets intensified at the time of puberty. One notices without fail that there are numerous exhortations to discipline the body of every girl who attains her age. It is not uncommon to hear such exhortations as: "Sit properly"; "keep the legs together"; "don't lie down on your back"; "eat little"; "don't go out to play with boys"; "don't stand near the door"; "walk modestly with head bent"; "laugh softly", etc. These orders are usually passed on either by a grandmother, aunt or mother or by an elder sister.

In an unstructured interview Kavitha, spoke out, "I am very careful, especially when I appear in public. I talk softly. Otherwise people will suspect my character." It was also obvious that a woman's body is subjected to a still finer discipline while sitting or waiting for a train or bus. They take as little space as possible with arms close to the bodies, hands folded together on their laps, toes pointing straight ahead or turned inward, and legs pressed together. Even while sleeping women mostly lie on one side and not on their back.

21. Aṭakkam means bodily modesty and docility.

In a focused group discussion at Vedasandur, women opined that a 'good'[22] woman avoids the male gaze. They also spoke of many proverbs that encourage women to discipline their bodies.

To cite a few examples, accamum, maṭamum, nāṇamum, payirppum niccamum peṇpārkkuriyatu which means fear, ignorance, shyness and sobriety all belong to women. Another common proverb says, pompaḷa ciriccā pōccu: pokayila viricca pōccu meaning a laughing woman is equal to a tobacco that has lost its essence by opening out. Such views underscore the link between women's bodily behavior and morality.[23] The stress on morality and decorous behavior of women is not just a pre-marital requirement, but operates both before and after marriage, involving both personal and familial honor. Even after marriage, a woman's body is under constant supervision by society as well as by the family, and very often by the husband himself.

The respondents also insisted upon bodily modesty through tying of their hair especially when they go out, or when they are in the presence of men and elders. For instance, a young girl can have a short hair. But after seven or eight years it must be oiled, plaited, and allowed to hang down at the back as a braid. The author came across very few girls leaving their hair loose while the majority of them went around in plaited hair. The various disciplinary controls on woman's body leading them to docility and submissiveness deprive them of autonomy over their body.

Devika 42, a college professor, said, "Women must be very careful in public. They must discipline their body at all levels. I am very particular to bring up my girl child properly. Because a family is judged by the way they bring up the girl-child and the way ṭhe girl-child behaves. Otherwise, it will affect our kuṭumpa kauravam. In order to safeguard our kuṭumpa kauravam, we abide by the expectations of our society."

Such a statement indicates the nexus between the disciplining of a woman's body and kuṭumpa kauravam in Tamil culture. However, when it comes to preoccupation with kuṭumpa kauravam, a significant difference is seen among those who are economically well off and those who are at the lower strata of society. The data shows that 82 percent of the

22. Here the word 'good' denotes the moral life of a person.

23. Katie Conboy writes in her book that physical movement of women must exhibit not only constriction but also grace and certain eroticism, restrained by modesty. Cf. Conboy et al., eds., *Writing on the Body*, 135–36.

respondents who are economically well-off are concerned about their kuṭumpa kauravam, whereas in the case of respondents from the lower strata of society, it was only 32 percent.

As the level of economic means of the respondents increases, there is a simultaneous growth in anxiety towards the preservation of their kuṭumpa kauravam. This brings to light how in spite of the higher education and status in society, kuṭumpa kauravam takes precedence over women's self-perception of the body. Analysis also indicates the link between the female body and kuṭumpa kauravam.

Restraint vs. Resistance

The respondents' perceptions on bodily aṭakkam disclose that not all follow what society exhorts them to do. It was evident that women in unorganized sectors seem to be more courageous in refusing to live up to the expectations of society than those in organised sectors.

For example, in an in-depth interview Kali 35, who is an unorganized laborer, said, "I do not bother about what society tells me or thinks of me. It determines my behavior and dictates how I should hold my body in public. But I do not follow it. It's my life and I would live my life in the way I want. Sometimes people speak ill of me. But I do not bother about it." In another context Anjamma, asked, "If we are going to be bothered about what society might think of us, then our stomach will go empty. Who will feed our family? Will my society feed our family? Will kuṭumpa kauravam fill our empty stomachs? So I am not bothered about what society thinks of me."

71 percent of the respondents who work in unorganized sectors opined that they go against the regulations of society when it does not serve them whereas in the case of organized sectors it is only 34 percent.

Analysis of the data indicates that when it is a matter of daily living and survival, women simply ignore kuṭumpa kauravam and even do not hesitate to go against the expectations of society. Thus for women who mostly work in unorganized sector, survival is much more important than kuṭumpa kauravam.

In the same way, a difference is seen among those live in rural areas and in urban settings. 52 percent of the respondents, who live in urban centers, said that they do not bother about what society thinks of them.

This indicates that there is a variation among respondents based on their geographical location.

But with regard to the data on women's attitude towards living up to the expectations of society, the analysis does not show any remarkable difference among respondents on the basis of education, economic status and age group.

What emerges from the above investigation is that women's attitude towards fulfilling the expectations of society depends on one's need for survival and exposure. Thus the analysis seems to indicate that the matter of survival plays a greater role in women's understanding of their body. Besides, exposure to urban life helps women to exercise their autonomy and freedom with regard to their body to a certain extent. When exposed into new spaces, women meet with the people of different cultures, religions, communities and languages. New space brings with it new relationships, opening them up to a world with a new outlook and new way of dealing with the self and the body. As a result, their traditional approach towards the body changes and the inhibition about it begins to diminish.[24]

THE BODY AND THE DRESS CODE

Another perception with regard to the female body centers on women's dress code. A woman is expected to cover her body properly all the time, especially her sexual organs. It was evident in the research area that from the age five onwards, girls are seen in long skirts flowing down to their ankles and in a long type of blouse. After puberty, the girl is swathed in a half- sari,[25] which adds to the long skirt, while a light cloth covers the girl's breasts. And the sari is wound completely around the female body to mark the transition from the free and unencumbered stage of girlhood to womanhood. A particular emphasis is placed on training girls to be aware at all times to ensure that the top of the sari cover their breasts—even while engaged in physically demanding tasks.

Very few young girls and young women in the town and urban centers like Dindigul and Kodai Kanal, and still fewer in rural areas, are

24. Foucault has argued that the transition from traditional to modern societies has been characterized by a profound transformation in the exercise of power, which he calls "a reversal of the political axis of individualization." See Foucault, *Discipline and Punish*, 44.

25. Sari is an Indian woman's costume. It is normally five and a half meters long.

seen wearing *salwar kameez.*[26] The freedom of dress is tolerated to some extent before marriage. After marriage in the semi-urban areas very few use *salwar kameez.* In the villages, most married women wear only sari.

Mathi Selvi a housewife of 45, said, "Women are the cause for men's misbehavior. If a woman dresses properly, men will not be tempted to abuse them. She must cover her body properly, especially her breasts, so that no one is sexually aroused while looking at her." Ranjini 39, a nurse in a private clinic said, "Our culture expects women to cover their body properly. If a woman does not cover her body properly, it will not be considered decent, and she can easily be harassed. I am very careful to see that my body is covered properly."

Such perceptions were not that of Ranjini and Mathi Selvi only but also of 54 percent of the women interviewed. This is an example of the trivial way in which conservatism in dress continues to shape the ideas of what is decent and indecent.

The facts reveal that two factors namely *culture* and *religion* seem to contribute strongly towards women's traditional perception of the dress code. According to some of the respondents, 'covering the body has something to do with Tamil culture.' Hence, they consider it as very important to preserve cultural practices regarding their dress code. 62 percent of the total respondents said that they preserve their culture by wearing the traditional sari.

In the same way, 79 percent of the Muslim respondents said that they wear purdah[27] because they are instructed by their religion to do so. Shameema Begum 36, said, "In fact I want to wear a convenient dress. But according to our religion, women have to cover their body completely with purdah. If I do not cover my body, my husband will scold me or punish me. So, I am afraid to remove it." This reveals that in their attempt to preserve and fulfill traditional and religious practices, Muslim women are deprived of autonomy even to choose the dress that they want to wear.

26. *Salwar kameez* is a North Indian woman's costume. Nowadays it is being used by women all over India.

27. Purdah is a kind of outer garment, used by Muslim women, to cover their face and their body.

Rewriting the Dress Code

All the same, some of the Muslim respondents had also a difference of opinion with regard to their dress. Especially there was a significant difference seen on the basis of their occupation. The Muslim women, who work in unorganized sectors, were much more daring in removing their purdah than women in organized sectors.

For instance Mehaboob 39, said:

> I am a cittāḷ. I carry cement, bricks and other things on my head. My work demands that I do away with the purdah. If I am particular to follow the teachings of religion regarding purdah, then I will not be able to work. When I do not work, we cannot survive. So work is more important than purdah. So I do not feel bad about it also. I feel bad only when I am unable to work and earn.

32 percent of the Muslim respondents who work in unorganized sectors expressed similar views while it was only 12 percent of those who work in organized sectors said that they remove their purdah.

As the data on women's perception of space has already brought to light, it is mostly housewives who tend to hold on to the traditions of one's religious practices rather than those who move into society for work. However, a deeper analysis demonstrates that when it is a matter of economic survival, women exercise their agency to throw away even their religious customs and practices that bind them through dress code. Muslim women who work in organized sectors were rather found hesitant to remove their purdah as in the case of Shameema Begum for fear of being punished by their religion or given a divorce notice. This indicates that in spite of their higher education and placement in society, these women do not seem to be assertive in exercising their autonomy.

Besides, some of the respondents belonging to Hindu and Christian religions, but who were mostly highly educated and employed, said that they do not go by what society expects of them; rather they wear the dress which is convenient to them. Among them, 21 percent said that they wear *salwaar kameez* always, in spite of opposition.

Priya 35, a post-graduate, said:

> I have to go daily from my village to work in an office in Madurai (a nearby city). I find it very difficult to travel with a sari in a crowded bus. So I use only *salwaar kameez*. People sometimes make comments about it, but I do not care. Because ultimately I have to decide what I want in life. If I want always people's good

> opinion, I cannot be what I am. I prefer to be free and comfortable with myself than to be bothered about what others are saying about me.

Thus, for some of the women who work in organized sectors or who are financially sound, convenience comes first in deciding the dress they wear.

Tāimai Aṭaital [28]

Another predominant perception that prevailed among the women respondents with regard to their body was to attain the state of motherhood. In fact, woman's body gains its significance on the day when it proves to the world that it can produce. It is surprising to note that so much emphasis is laid on the woman as a child-bearer.

Body and Fertility

The attitude that the female body is meant to bring forth a child is seen right at the time of the puberty of the girl. In one of the research areas, the author observed how the pubescent girl was fed with good food to strengthen her body, especially to strengthen her uterus and waist in order to bring forth a healthy child in a normal or safest way possible. Food regulations thus serve to regulate the menstrual cycle and strengthen the reproductive organs, underlining the dominant perception of the female body as oriented to reproduction.

It is noteworthy that the custom of celebrating the first menstruation of every girl is a public ritual occasion, signaling to the community the actual transition made from girlhood to womanhood. More revealing is the usage when a girl attains puberty: periya manuṣi āyiṭṭā—she has become a woman. This signifies the readiness of a girl's body for marriage and fertility, which is another vital idea surrounding menstruation, apart from the notion of pollution.

It was noticeable that once a woman completes two or three months of her married life, she faces innumerable questions like "Any good news?" "Is he OK?" "Any problem?" "Did you consult the doctor?" The author also witnessed women undertaking a series of pilgrimages to propitiate the gods and goddesses, so that they may bless their womb with a fetus, especially with a male fetus. Whether early or late, a woman

28. Tāimai Aṭaital means to attain the state of motherhood.

is bound to prove her ability to give birth to a child. Many are of the opinion that motherhood makes woman a complete being. A sense of relief is seen when a woman becomes pregnant for the first time.

Gomathi said, "In fact, I did not want to give birth to a child immediately. I wanted to wait for five years. But people started asking me and making me feel bad about it. They even began to wonder whether I am having a good relationship with my husband at all. So, in order to do away with all kinds of comments, I had to give birth to a child within two years."

In a focused group discussion women opined, "Whoever she may be, first of all a woman must bring forth a child." 69 percent of the respondents irrespective of religion, caste, occupation and age group expressed the idea that a woman's body attains the state of fullness only when it gives birth to children. Such an outlook clearly underlines women's internalization of social conditionings regarding married women to prove their fertility by bringing forth children.

All the same, among the total respondents, 31 percent of them had a different outlook towards motherhood. The responses of Kanjana and Amali are more enlightening in this context.

For instance, in an in-depth interview Kanjana 37, a post-graduate and a Hindu, said:

> It is true that my body is meant to bring forth children and to find fulfillment in it. But bringing forth children is not everything in life. It is only one phase of my bodily achievement. My body is also capable of achieving many more things in life. I do not want to end my life by just being a mother of two children. So, even when my husband told me not to go for work, I refused to be at home as merely a wife and a mother; rather I took up work in order to make use of my bodily abilities.

In the same way, Amali 35, a soft-ware engineer by profession and a Christian, said, "Of course, as soon as I got married, my family members wanted me to bring forth a child and prove to the world that I am fertile. But I decided to contribute something to the world before I bring forth a child. So, I did not give birth for seven years. I had to hear all sorts of calumnies. My in-laws spoke ill of me. But I did not give up my decision to delay."

It is surprising to note that as the educational level of the respondent increases, their desire for motherhood is decreasing. For example,

87 percent of illiterate and those who have completed primary level of school and 72 percent of those who have completed higher secondary level expressed the view that motherhood is very important for a woman, whereas among those highly qualified, it was only 41 percent.

In the same way, a noteworthy disparity is seen among respondents based on their geographical locations also. Only 51 percent of the respondents from the urban setting opined that they consider motherhood as very essential for them, while in the case of respondents from the rural area, it was 84 percent.

Further, the investigation on the data does not show any significant difference in their attitude towards motherhood on the basis of caste, occupation and economical status. Thus the above data throws some light on the impact of education and the geographical location of the respondents with regard to their understanding of motherhood.

This indicates that there is a changing trend taking place among educated and urban women with regard to their role of motherhood. The above mentioned factors seem to help women in recognizing their bodily abilities beyond motherhood. Consequently women are slowly beginning to refuse to accept passively the societal outlook on their bodies as vessels meant to carry *only babies.*

Body and Barrenness

The inability to conceive, as well as to bear a male child is viewed as failures for which the woman's body is generally held accountable and treated as a curse. In the case of infertility, it is usually the woman who is termed malati or barren.[29]

In an in-depth interview, Sudha 32, a separated wife shared her experience of living with the stigma of being a wife who had no issue. She said, "Although I earn and bring a salary to my house, since I have no issue, I am considered as a curse in my family. I usually do not take part in any auspicious ceremonies. I do not know what sin I have committed? Why is this curse on me?" 64 percent of the responses brought to light that even if a woman's body is capable of many other things, it is still considered as an "unproductive" one, when it has not brought forth

29. From the field observance and from in-depth interviews it was very evident that most men are reluctant to test themselves for possible sexual inadequacies. It is not so much through fear as through a sense of outrage at the implication that their virility is being questioned. Hence a woman's body is easily victimized.

a child. As far as the society is concerned, female infertility is a humiliation to the woman even today.

Nevertheless, the field observation and data also disclosed something different from the conventional views. Some of the barren women were taking part in auspicious occasions like cīmantam and marriage ritual. For instance, Kala said, "What is there to feel bad about it? It can happen to anyone. Especially, if a woman is not able to bring forth a child, it is not her fault. When any part of our body does not function well, do we call our body, a curse? Then why this curse, only for womb?"

In another incident, Malathi 29, the second daughter-in-law of her house, who has two children and who is given the status of being cumaṅkali, is used to the different treatment meted out to her family's first daughter-in-law Kannagi who is barren. When the third son in the house was getting married, by custom it is the cumaṅkali who performs all the ceremonies during the celebration. But to everyone's surprise and shock, Malathi brought in Kannagi to perform the rite. Kannagi was the main person to do all the traditional rituals.

When asked, Malathi said:

> Sometime you have to start breaking the age-old ideas about women. It is women who have to do it and not men. The new couple's future does not depend on the woman who performs the rite, rather on the couple's hard work and commitment to each other. It is usually believed that only when the cumaṅkali blesses the marriage the couple will have a bright future. If it is so, then, are all the couples blessed by a cumaṅkali, happy and prosperous? Anyone who is good at heart is worthy of blessing another. It does not depend on whether she is productive or barren, widow or a prostitute.

Such assertive statements and actions underscore how women are beginning to think differently and question the existing perception and attitude of society regarding the barren womb.

When we look at the respondents' attitude towards barren women, a significant variation can be observed among the respondents based on their occupation and economic status. 32 percent of the housewives and 42 percent of those who work in organized sector opined that they treat barren women in a normal way, while in the case of respondents who work in unorganized sectors, it was 89 percent. Thus the respondents who work in unorganized sectors score higher than the other groups.

Similarly the figures show a remarkable difference among the respondents based on their economic status. 72.4 percent of those who earn lower than Rs. 2000 ($43) and 61.1 percent of those who earn between Rs. 2000–5000 ($43—$107) opined that they treat the barren women in a normal way, while among those who are economically well-off, it was only 42.4 percent.

The scrutiny of the data indicates that respondents employed in the unorganized sector and those who economically come from the lower strata of society seem to treat barren women in a normal way. The analysis also shows that as the level of economic means increases, there is a corresponding decrease in treating barren women as normal human beings. Thus the study brings to light that treating the barrenness of a woman's body as something lacking is found more among women who are well-off, than among the lower strata of society.

Moreover, a significant difference is seen among the respondents on the basis of their involvement in action-oriented groups. Only 42 percent of those who are involved in action-oriented groups said that their body finds fulfillment solely in giving birth to children, while, among those who have no influence of such groups, it was 82 percent. To cite an example, Roja 39, said, "I felt very sad and ashamed when I heard that I cannot bring forth a child. I used to avoid the public. But after joining DEEPAM,[30] I am made to realize that my body is of much more worth than just bringing forth children."

Analysis of the above data clearly indicates the impact of action-oriented groups on the perception of these women regarding motherhood. These groups have played a role of empowerment in conscientizing the respondents to acknowledge their bodily abilities beyond the womb. Through the different awareness programs conducted in the groups, women are helped to explode the taboos surrounding barren women. They have been also initiated to decode the metaphor which favors only those women who can bear children and in particular, male children, thus freeing them from the so-called feminine ideologies.[31]

30. It is an NGO that works for the empowerment of women.

31. B. R. Siwal observes that women's movements in India have played a crucial role in creating awareness among men and women and uplifting the status of women. Siwal, "Women's Movement in India," 4–7. Cf. also Gandhi and Nandita, *The issues at stake.*

Kaṟpu[32]

Kaṟpu is another perception that surrounds woman's body. This is apparent in the way a girl / a woman is treated in society when raped or mishandled by a man. The phrase kaṟpu aḻiñcu pōccu signifies that a woman has lost her chastity.

Kaṟpu *and Bodily Purity*

Treating bodily purity as chastity is very common among Tamils. In one of the focused group discussions, the respondents opined that women must at all cost preserve their bodies from being touched or molested by men. Especially, they must be pure both before and after their marriage.

In this context Rupa 35, a Christian by religion, said, "Even if the husband goes after another, a woman must remain faithful to the marital commitment. Whatever it may be, a woman must be chaste by keeping her body pure. By being chaste, she brings blessings to the family and especially to her husband. It is a power for women. But if something happens to her body, her family's reputation will be at stake."

This was not the opinion of Rupa only; there were also other women who were of the same opinion. These perceptions underscore women's internalization of marital commitment as one of bodily purity,[33] which is linked to the life, and prosperity of the family. Chastity itself is considered as a source of power and a social recognition for women.[34]

Another related perception that emerged from women's understanding of chastity had to do with the ownership of woman's body. For instance Kavitha said, "In the case of rape or any type of sexual harassment, the man who touches the woman, must marry her and make her his wife." Respondents irrespective of religion, caste, economic status opined that the man who touches the woman's body first must become the owner of that body.

32. Kaṟpu *is a Tamil word for chastity*

33. This fixation with body-purity and loyalty to the marital bond may not be a unique phenomenon peculiar only to Tamil region. It could be seen in other regions too. However, the easy acceptability of this notion and the undue reverence and constant reference to it in an obsessive manner is typical of Tamils. Suresh Nambath also shares the same opinion. See Nambath, "A Freedom at Stake . . . ," 1.

34. David Dean Shulman speaks about this element of chastity of a married woman which is expressed in total devotion to her husband. The life of a husband is felt literally dependent upon the sacred power vested in his wife. For further details, see Shulman, *Tamil Temple Myths*, 140.

For example, Kannamma 42, owner of a big estate in Kodai Kanal said, "A woman must remain faithful to her husband always even if he goes astray. Bodily purity is something special to Tamil culture. Kannagi[35] is portrayed as a model for all of us. Therefore, we have the duty to preserve our culture. It depends on women's behaviour whether the culture is kept up or not."

With regard to respondents' attitude towards kaṟpu, a significant difference is seen based on their religion and economic status. 72 percent of women who are economically well-off opined that a chaste woman must preserve her bodily purity, while among women who are economically in the lower strata of society, it was only 43 percent. This brings to light that the traditional perception regarding kaṟpu is stronger among women who are economically well off than among respondents from the lower strata of society.

Thus, the analysis on the data reveals that as women grow higher in economic status, their focus of bodily purity also gets stronger. This indicates that the economically well to do seem to be engaged with the preservations of traditions and culture even at the cost of their autonomy. Nevertheless, for women who live below the poverty line, the concern of survival is much more a daunting issue than preserving bodily purity.

Likewise, a considerable variation is identified among the respondents of different religions. 64 percent of Christian respondents expressed that women must preserve bodily purity, while in the case of Hindus and Muslims, it was only 32 percent and 41 percent respectively. To cite an example, Rachel 41, one of the Christian respondents said, "We are taught by our religion that we should keep our body pure. Hence, at all costs, we must preserve bodily purity. I feel guilty when I fail in this." The facts clearly indicate that Christian women score high for their traditional attitude towards kaṟpu than the respondents of other religions.

However, it is striking that the perception of bodily purity as chastity is found stronger among women who are regular churchgoers than among those who go rarely to church. The respondents who rarely go to church seem to have a different opinion. Such findings bring to light the elements of agency in the perceptions of Christian women who do not visit church regularly. One of the reasons could be the negative impact of Christian teaching on body and sexuality.

35. One of the Tamil epics Cilappatikāram speaks about Kannagi. She is considered as Kaṟpukkaraci (queen of chastity) (queen of chastity) and portrayed as the role model of chastity for every Tamil woman.

Kaṟpu *and Marital Loyalty*

Women are expected by culture and religion to remain faithful to their husbands even when the husbands are disloyal to them. The data on women's understanding of marital loyalty discloses a significant difference among the respondents based on their involvement in action-oriented groups. For instance, Kalai Vani said:

> Although I earn and take care of my family, I used to be afraid of my husband. He had a ciṉṉa vīṭu *(concubine)* also. I tolerated his behavior just because I was told to put up with everything. After joining DEEPAM[36] I have become aware of the oppressive situation of women in the name of pati viratāi (wifely loyalty). DEEPAM also stands by me in my decisions. Now, I am bold to tell my husband that what he is doing is wrong. I tell him plainly to remain committed, or else to leave me for good. I am not frightened to live alone.

In an in-depth interview, Deepa, a Christian who goes to church once a month or two, but a regular attendant of POORNA[37] said:

> We cannot be like Kannagi anymore. The days have gone when women waited for their husbands to return after loafing around. My husband is a drunkard and he has a ciṉṉa vīṭu. I know that he was going regularly to her, spending all his earnings on her. I pretended as if I was unaware of his behavior. Now and then he used to come home, pretending to be sick. My children used to scold me for keeping silence over the whole issue. One day he suddenly disappeared from the scene for two years. I came to know that he was living with his ciṉṉa vīṭu. People came advising me to bring him back to my home. The priest in our local church advised me to bear up with everything for Christ' sake. It looked funny. Why should I go to bring him? This is his life. If he finds his life and happiness there, let him live there. So, I did not bother to call him back, or cry over this issue. To our sụrprise, after two years, one fine day he returned to me. I told him plainly, 'get out' and showed him the door. I prefer to live alone than to live with a man who is uncommitted.

Such assertive responses indicate that in a soil where usually men 'demand' their women to be pure while taking their chastity for granted,

36. It is an NGO that works for the empowerment of women.

37. It is a Palani based NGO that works for the empowerment of Dalits and women.

women demanding 'their men' to be pure and committed are indeed a clear indication of agency. Besides, the whole understanding of marriage from the side of women as one of tolerance in case of abuse and disloyalty is also taking a different turn. They prefer to live alone when met with disloyalty on the part of their husbands. It was striking to note that among the respondents who are involved in action-oriented groups, 62 percent of them said that they would prefer to live alone than to live with an uncommitted man.

Unlike their attitude towards motherhood, educational qualification and occupation of the respondents do not have a considerable impact on their understanding of kaṟpu and pati viratāi. But the impact of action-oriented groups is a positive factor in their understanding of kaṟpu and pati viratāi.

According to the analysis, the impact of action-oriented groups in the lives of these women is greater than higher education. It has empowered them to take control of their lives in situations of abuse or disloyalty and to deconstruct the traditional myths of chastity and pati viratāi.[38] The above finding suggests that women need to be empowered not merely economically and educationally but also socially and culturally.

BODY AS tīṭṭu[39]

Female body as tīṭṭu is one of the predominant perceptions of women, mostly at the time of menstruation and at childbirth. Though the first menstruation is in itself an auspicious event in the life of a woman, yet the menstruating body is considered tīṭṭu and polluting.[40]

38. The above finding of the present study is in conformity with what Pippa Norris writes. He says that women's movement has been more successful in changing attitudes towards sexual equality. For more information, see Norris, Politics & Sexual Equality, 132.

39. Tīṭṭu means impure.

40. Other studies have led to similar observations. Cf. S. Wadley, *The Powers Of Tamil Women*, 40–41; Bagwe, *Of Woman Caste*, 198; The anthropological studies in many countries and cultures, both in the modern and ancient world, show that among the most primitive as well as the most civilized peoples, menstruation was and still is connected with ideas of danger, shame and sin. Cf. Deutsch, *The Psychology of Women*, 152. All the same, menstruation, a biological aspect of woman's body, does not have a universal meaning applicable to all cultures. That is why after studying theories of menstrual symbolism, Thomas Buckley and Alma Gottileb could conclude, "above all, menstrual taboos are cultural constructions and must be approached as such—symbolic, arbitrary, contextualized and potentially multivalent—whose meanings emerge only

It is apparent in the way the women respondents inform one another during their monthly menstruation. They customarily use the phrases like nāṉ cuttamā illai (I am not clean) or nāṉ tīṭṭā irukkēṉ (I am impure), etc. Māmiyā vantuṭṭā (Mother-in-law has come) is another customary expression among some of the youngsters, which has the same connotation as 'the arrival of an unwanted guest.'

The in-depth interview with Devika confirmed that the whole celebration of the puberty rite is preoccupied with the purification of the girl, the house and even the village. She said:

> I still remember that day of pūppuṉita nīrāṭṭu viḻā (Celebration for Puberty). From the time I came of age, I was asked to remain in a thatched hut for 16 days. The day previous to the real celebration, our house was whitewashed. On the completion of the 16th day, my mother's brother along with some men came early morning before sunrise, removed the coconut leaves and the bamboo poles used for the hut, took them to the outskirts of the village and burnt them. Meanwhile my aunties and other village women gave me a solemn turmeric bath. Then I was given a new set of clothes to wear, made to sit on a decorated chair which was placed in the middle of the pantal, put up just in front of our house for the ceremony and for the guests to sit. All eyes were on me. They performed rituals of which I understood nothing at that time. Some gave me gifts. Of course, I did get rest and a lot of attention during those days. What is humiliating is that I was kept away, not out of concern for my body but because it was impure.

Whether whitewashing the house, burning the leaves and the poles used for the hut, or giving bath to a girl, all signify only one thing: turning something impure into pure.

I observed that the notion of tīṭṭu is also insinuated in the ceremony of vaṇṇāṉ māttu.[41] As soon as the girl attains puberty, the family hangs neem leaves at the entrance of the house to inform the community/society about their state of impurity. The dress that she happens to wear on her puberty day is given to the *vaЇЇ ì*.[42] In some places, the pubescent girl is asked to wear the clothes borrowed from the dhobi during those *isolated* days. In some places, the girl is asked to wear it just for a day.

---

within the contexts of the fields of representations in which they exist." Cf. Buckley and A. Gottileb, *Blood Magic*, 24.

41. Vaṇṇāṉ māttu means exchange of clothes from a washerwoman.

42. A vaṇṇāṉ /*a dhobi* is one who washes the clothes of the people in the locality.

This kind of exchange of dress during the first menstruation a girl is called vaṇṇāṉ māttu, which means *exchange of clothes provided by dhobi.* This is mainly done as a custom to remove tīṭṭu (impurity) by another tīṭṭu. Vaṇṇāṉ – a dhobi - belongs to an untouchable community. The belief is that a menstruating girl who is considered as tīṭṭu *is helped to remove her* tīṭṭu by a dhobi who is also considered as tīṭṭu. If the tīṭṭu is not removed, it can cause great danger to the family and to the welfare of the village. So the symbolically takes the tīṭṭu from the pubescent girl by accepting the soiled clothes of the same. By this act, the girl's family is saved from tīṭṭu, and in turn regains its original position in their community/society.

Like the first menstruation, a woman's body during her first pregnancy is also considered tīṭṭu. The phrase muḻugāma irukkā meaning that *she has not bathed* is referred to a pregnant woman. This signifies not only the pregnant woman's physical impurity, but also her social and cultural impurity. Similarly, among some Hindu communities, a woman's body is considered impure from the time of delivery until purification. Her whole family too is considered impure. When people come to visit the mother and the child they do not enter the house but stand out and inquire after the mother and the new born babe. They do not even drink water from the house, since the whole household is deemed impure. On a fixed day, the mother and child are given a solemn bath and the whole house is whitewashed, in order to indicate the purity of the family. In some communities, especially after the birth of the offspring, women do undertake cooking as usual, but maintain a distance from the pūja (prayer) room.

In an unstructured interview Karthika, 33, a Hindu said, "In our caste we do not enter the house for sixteen days when a girl attains puberty as well as when a woman gives birth to a child. Because they are shedding 'impure' blood, the whole house is impure." Such a statement derives from the perception that the bloodshed at the time of menstruation as well as child-birth is dirty and a matter of shame. Therefore, women's responses and understanding of menstruation and child-birth is linked not so much to their own experiences of bodily changes, but to ideas of impurity.[43] This also gets extended to the notion of the patriarchal cultures that connect weakness, inferiority and shame to women's normal physical features and make women powerless.

43. Niranjana also makes a similar observation in her field study in the villages of Karnataka. Cf. Niranjana, *Gender and Space*, 60.

Body and māta vilakku

Māta vilakku *means isolation or separation during the monthly menstruation. The concept of female body as* tīṭṭu *during* menstruation leads to the isolation of menstruating women from their daily routines.[44]

Each community or caste of the respondents follows their custom and tradition to keep their women isolated during monthly menstruation.[45] More revealing is the usage vīṭṭukku tūramā irukaa (she is distanced from the house). In some areas women use phrases like vīṭṭukku tūramā irukkeṉ (I am away from the house).

Ponnamma 37, said:

> In our place, our neighbor[46] did not want to inform the community when her daughter came of age. Her daughter went about as usual without remaining separate. None of us knew about it except her mother-in-law. After a month, her husband met with a road accident and died on the spot. Immediately the accident was associated with the wife's attitude towards puberty. The mother-in-law started shouting standing in front of the house, "I knew this beforehand. Something might befall us. Āttā[47] will not be happy if we don't follow these rituals strictly. I told my daughter-in-law to follow the custom but she did not follow it. That's why my son has become a of āttā's anger.

44. This isolation starts right at the arrival of the first menstrual flow of a woman's body. It is effected by the actual or symbolic construction of a small hut made out of coconut leaves just outside the house, or in the place fixed by the village. The pubescent girl is not allowed to go anywhere during those days. She receives a warning from the family, mostly from the mother or aunt or grandmother to remain within the house. During menstruation, the girl's body is believed to be in a particularly heated and polluting condition. Measures are taken, therefore, to make sure that pollution does not spread and the heat does not become excessive.

45. During first menstruation, some remain isolated for nine days, others for 11 days, some others for 16 days or even for 30 days. The place of isolation differs from community to community. Some remain inside the house, some, in front of the house (at the right side) and some, in the place fixed by the village. The isolated woman is mostly given a separate plate, tumbler, and a mat to use during those days. In some communities, women continue this practice of isolating themselves from the normal stream of life during their monthly menstrual days. Although the celebration of puberty rite is held both in the Christian and Hindu communities (Muslims do not celebrate), the practice of monthly isolation during menstruation is prevalent only among the Hindus.

46. The neighbor whom the interviewee was referring to, is a person actively involved in women's movements.

47. Āttā means 'mother.' It is also used to address Hindu goddess.

In an in-depth interview, Kanthamma 39, an educated Dalit, said, "A menstruating body is impure, unholy and powerful. Therefore, it has to be kept away from all sacred things. I instruct my daughters to remain separate during those days. I don't allow them to go especially near plantain and neem trees. I am very particular about it."

It was obvious not only from the sharing of Ponnamma and Kanthamma but also from other testimonies that women isolate their bodies from gods. Some of them do not go near the picture of gods and goddesses, while most of them avoid crossing the temple or visiting the temple during those days for fear of punishment. Such a perception underlines women's strong tendency to attribute any mishap to the failure of menstruating women to observe the rites of purification or isolation. 74 percent of the Hindu respondents said that they distance themselves from others, especially from sacred things and places for fear of being punished by gods and goddesses.

Besides, women, mostly in the rural areas and few in the urban centers, avoid going near rose plants, plantain and kaṟi-leaf[48] plants, fearing that these plants might die off.[49] Most severe isolation, namely restriction within the four walls of the home, occurs at very specific moments in a woman's life—during first menstruation and during pregnancy, especially from the sixth month onwards until the childbirth.

Māta viṭāy[50] *vs.* Tīṭṭu

There is a striking variation based on caste in respondents' attitude towards body as impure during menstruation and pregbody as tīṭṭu during body as tīṭṭu during menstruation and pregnancy is noticed to be stronger among the respondents of MBC and BC than among the Dalits.

48. It's a leaf used for cooking while seasoning any curry items.

49. While referring to Pliny's view Simone de Beauvoir writes that a menstruating woman ruins crops, destroys gardens, kills bees and turns wine into vinegar. She points out from the *British Medical Journal* (1878), which reports 'It is an undoubted fact that meat spoils when touched by menstruating women.' Moreover, a woman having *the curse* was forbidden entry into refineries in northern France in the early twentieth century on the grounds that she could cause the sugar to blacken. Cf. Beauvoir, *The Second Sex*, 180–81.

50. Māta viṭāy is another word used for monthly menstruation by some of the respondents.

For instance, Mala 40, one of the BC respondents said:

> In our caste, we are told that our bodies are impure during menstruation. Therefore, I am very particular to follow it. If you do not follow what others are doing, then you might be blamed when something happens in the village. In addition, the blame will be on your family. Moreover, our Hindu religion treats the body as impure during menstruation. It says that kaṉṉi tīṭṭu vīṭṭukku ākātu, kaṉṉi tīṭṭu kaṭavuḻukku ākātu.[51] If I do not follow rules of purity and impurity, the gods and goddesses might punish me. So I follow it strictly.

64 percent of BC and 59 percent of MBC respondents said that their body is impure during pregnancy and menstruation. In the case of Dalits, it was only 24 percent.

The above data indicates that when it comes to observation of the purity code, BCs and MBCs are more conscious of it than the Dalits who are considered by the Indian society as untouchables. Besides, this also brings to light women's internalization of patriarchal restrictions imposed on woman's body during menstruation through caste and religious customs, thus alienating women from their own bodily functions. The customs and habits of caste continue to play a stronger role in spite of the advent of modernity.

Similarly, a significant difference was seen among the respondents' perception on their body during menstruation based on their caste. 82 percent of the Dalit women said that they do not consider their bodies impure but rather feel proud about it during menstruation as well as child-birth. In the case of other castes, such a positive view was comparatively very low. For instance, 36 percent of BCs and 41 percent of MBCs said that they do not consider their bodies impure but rather feel proud of them. The responses of some of the Dalit respondents are revealing in this context.

For instance Rama 38, one of the Dalit respondents said:

> What is there to feel shy? Puberty celebration is a community celebration of the body's maturity. If this maturity does not take place in the woman's body, the human race would not continue. When a girl attains a mature age, she joins other women to continue the human race. Don't you think that it needs celebration? I felt happy on the day of my pūppuṉita nīrāṭṭu viḻā. I was fed well

51. It means that the impurity of the virgin is not good for the family and for God.

> during those days. People visited me and they brought sweets, flowers and gifts for me. I felt so great about myself, about my body. Men's body is never celebrated. May be it does not deserve celebration, whereas a woman's body needs and deserves celebration because it is so wonderful.

In a focused group discussion held at Mullipadi[52] the Dalit respondents said that they feel good and happy about menstruation. One of the members from the group by name Parvatiamma 41, said:

> How can our bodies be impure if we are created by God? Though society labels me impure, I am not so. I feel proud of my body and take good care of my body. I do not bother about what society thinks of me. I really love getting my menstruation. It's like the changing of seasons in nature. I feel a bond with nature and with other women. I feel fertile, womanly and empowered because of my potential to bring forth life. I even like the little aches I get because it's a reminder of having my period.

As the above data discloses, the responses from the Dalit women regarding their body during menstruation are highly remarkable. In spite of the oppressive status into which Dalit women are placed, they experience a sense of pride, happiness and a feeling of goodness about their own body during menstruation. Their awareness of the significance of menstruation for the continuation of the human community and their experience of being connected to the seasons of nature as well as to other women are something constructive.

BODY AS A SEXUAL OBJECT

The female body as a site or an object of sex is another perception that occupies the mind of the respondents. Most of them said that their body is treated as a sexual object meant to give pleasure to their husbands. Either at the time of marriage, or at the time of the visit of the young married girl to her maternal home, one often hears this oft-repeated phrase puruṣaṉa muntāṉaiyile muṭiñcu vaccukkō (tie your husband by the tip of your sari) which means keep your husband under your control by being generous in bed.

In an in-depth interview Kowsalya 35, said, "My aunt told me that I should be always pleasing to my husband. In fact, I try to satisfy him

52. Mullipadi is one of the villages in the research area.

in all ways possible. Then only he will not go after any other woman." Such a statement underlines the unwritten law that is accepted by all, or at least by the womenfolk. It is assumed that if the wife is not generous in bed, then her husband may look for another woman for his needs. Even when the wife is good and faithful, and if the husband goes after someone, mostly the wife is being blamed for failing in her duties of strī-tarmā.

Jyothi 35, a Christian said, "My body is just an object of pleasure for my husband. I have to maintain this object in good condition, so that my husband enjoys the maximum out of it. When I am not able to satisfy him sexually, I feel bad about it." Lakshmi 30, a Hindu confides, "After all, my body is created to give satisfaction to my husband. Just because he has tied a tāli I am forced to satisfy him even when I am not in a good disposition. There's no other go."

In a focused group discussion held at Oddanchatram, it was very evident from women's perspective that sexuality is nothing but submitting or surrendering their own desires and preferences in deference to their male partner.[53] Some of them said that they often accommodate to male sexual desire and feel dominated by it. Some others said that if they do not give in to their husbands' desires, then it might lead to unwanted anxiety and conflicts. As one woman told me, she does nothing that may awaken her husband at night as she is afraid that he might jump on her body once again.

Such perceptions unearth women's internalization of their body as an object created for man. They feel that they are obliged to give pleasure to their husbands always. Barring some isolated cases, there does not seem to be any change in women respondents' attitude to sex and to their body. 71 percent of the respondents said that their body is created for the pleasures of man.

Thus sexuality, for these women, is tinged with fear of the *other*'s body. It is also clear that sexuality is central to these women's definitions of femininity, and they appear to depend, to a large extent, on their partners for this aspect of their self-definition.

53. Rector has made a similar comment in his writings. Cf. "Are We Making Love Yet?," 74.

Female Body as Male Chattels

With regard to their understanding of body and sexuality, the respondents, irrespective of their religious background opined that they are taught by their religion to please their husbands always. Dorothy 32, a Christian said, "My religion teaches me that I should please my husband and obey him always, because women's bodies are created for the pleasures of men." Rohini 37, a Hindu said, "Our religious teachings instruct us to satisfy men. This is what we are expected to be and do when we marry a man. Otherwise, we will be spoken ill off, and our name will be spoiled." Katheeja Begum 35, a Muslim said, "We cannot even imagine that this body is ours. My husband constantly tells me that I should obey the teachings of the Quran by obeying him." This clearly demonstrates the vital role religion and its sacred scriptures play in the self-perception of women concerning their body. They have created in women a feeling of estrangement towards their body by making them continue to believe that man is the proprietor of their body.

However, amidst the oppressive views that perpetuate the colonization of woman's body in the name of marriage, there are women who defy the general perception. Analysis of the data shows that respondents' perception on sexuality is highly influenced by their age group.

Respondents in the age group of 21–30 take control of their body to a greater extent than those in other age groups. Irrespective of the religion they belong to, women in the age group of 21–30 were much more courageous than those in other age groups.

Sarala Devi 24, a Hindu, said, "One day my husband told me that I should do all that he tells me. I told him, 'I am sorry. Those days have gone. Things have changed. I am not your paid servant to do all that you tell me. I am your life-partner. I cannot live like an eternal slave. If you cannot treat me as a person, please keep this tāli with you, and look for another. I prefer to live a dignified life." Fatima Begum 27, a Muslim said, "Although my religion says that a woman's body is created for a man and we are to satisfy them at all levels, I don't give into his desire. I am not a dry stick to lie there all the time to satisfy him. When I say something, he is not very happy. But I cannot destroy my life for him."

In an unstructured interview, Fatima 25, a Christian[54] asserted, "It's my body. Nobody, not even my husband, has the right over this body

54. She is a housewife and a member of DMSSS (Dindigul Multi-purpose Social Service Society).

of mine. Sometimes, my husband keeps telling me that he has a right over my body, since he has tied the tāli. I answer back saying, 'this tāli is not a license for you to do anything to me, and if you hold on to this view, then better keep the tāli with you.'" Some of the young women whose husbands are alive even dare to go about without the tāli. Such courageous responses and actions highlight young women's audacity to re-claim their body and sexuality. They do not want to give their bodily freedom into the hands of men.

Thus, it is evident from the field that with regard to their sexuality, the young respondents are much more daring and dynamic than the older ones. Added to that, it was identified that 72 percent of the respondents in the age group of 21–30 said that they do not always give into the expectations of their husbands. They do not hesitate to walk out of the married life either. Apparently, this is due to the exposure to new and liberal thinking regarding sexuality which the respondents in their age group of 21–30 are experiencing.

Sex and Sexual Organs

It is obvious in the office or in the school staff room or in the field or in the flower garden, women do discuss a lot of topics—politics, cinema, beauty-care, clothes, and every other sundry topics, but never sex. The women are not only reluctant but also very cautious and careful to cover their bodies especially their sexual organs. They hesitate to use the right name for sexual organs also. Even when they happen to open the topic in close circles, it will be closed off as soon as they see someone approaching them.

However, according to the data, treating sex and sexual organs as something shameful, evil and sinful is stronger among Christian women than among the women of other religions. The responses of three Christian participants in this context are revealing.

Mary, a teacher and a Christian by religion, said:

> I was brought up to believe that it is a sin to touch or even to look at or mention my private parts. I grew up hating my own physical imperfections. I wore my body with much shame, fear and hate because of all the stereotypes imposed on it. A good woman and a normal housewife will not speak about sex. Only a loose woman will be interested in this topic. Moreover, sex is the topic for men. I feel ashamed if someone talks to me about sex.

Elisabeth 38, a housewife and regular church-goer, said, "A good and holy woman will not speak about sex. It is men's area. Only a loose woman will talk about sex. I never talk about sex, because talking about sex is a sin." Theresa 42, a regular attendant of church activities, said, "Every time I have a sexual relationship with my husband, I go to confession. My body leads me to sin. This body is a burden. So I hate my body. I do not like to be a woman."

Among the total respondents, 72 percent of the Christian respondents consider sex as evil and sinful, whereas only 32 percent of Hindus and 41 percent of Muslims said that sex is evil. The figures demonstrate a noticeable difference among the respondents of different religions with regard to their attitude towards sex.

A deeper analysis of the data shows that the tendency of treating sex as evil and sinful is found more among the Christian respondents who are very regular for church activities than among those who go to church rarely. For example, among the Christian respondents who consider sex as evil, 82 percent of them were regular church-goers, whereas in the case of those who never go to church, it was only 21 percent.

Furthermore, the analysis does not show any remarkable difference in their understanding of sex on the basis of education or employment.

Hence, what emerges from the above analysis is that women's understanding of sex and sexuality *depends to a greater extent on the teachings of one's religion.* There seems to be some link between their attitude towards sexuality and the respective religion to which one belongs. This is a clear indication of the impact of the traditional and narrow understanding of Christianity concerning sex and sexuality, which continues to linger on in the minds of the Christian faithful, in spite of their higher education and occupation.

Body and Sexual Needs

All the same, there are some who come forward to say that they feel comfortable with their body; they do discuss the issues concerning sex and sexuality with their husbands and friends. For example, Karthigai 35, a housewife and a daily viewer of TV channels said, "In the beginning I used to feel ashamed of and feel shy to talk about sex. But after watching the daily programmes on the TV, now I consider that sex is not something dangerous which I should run away from, or consider a sin. Rather it is a part of me."

In another context, Janaki 35, said, "In fact, we are not supposed to take the initiative or express our need for sex. A woman can ask from her husband a sari, a gold jewel, or money but not intimacy. Very often a woman who asks for sex will be looked down upon. It is mostly the man who decides when and how. But I don't feel a hesitation to express my need for intimacy. This is my body. I am aware of its needs."

Poorani 31, said, "I used to feel ashamed of my body. I was completely ignorant of my sexuality. After reading books and watching different television channels I have become aware of my body and sexuality. Now, I don't feel shy or ashamed of my body. In fact I appreciate my body and its beauty. I freely relate with my husband. I even discuss matters of sex with him."

According to the data on the respondents' understanding of sex, a remarkable difference could be noticed among those who view the media regularly and those who rarely or never view the media. 42 percent of the respondents who are regular viewers of the media said that they take the initiative to express their bodily and sexual needs, while in the case of those who view them once a week and rarely, it was only 12 and 3 percent respectively.

Analysis of the data indicates the affirmative role of the media in freeing women from inhibition and from a sense of shame around their body and sexuality. By bringing to the fore the areas (regarding sex) that have been hidden for centuries, the media is also slowly enabling women to break the conventional understanding of sex as men's domain.

Likewise, a significant variation was observed by me among the respondents on the basis of their age group. To cite an example, Vimala, 24 said, "What is there to feel shy about? The media brings out everything openly. I read a lot. My friends also share with me. So, I do not feel ashamed to share my sexual needs with my husband or with my friends. This is my body. And I feel good about it when I come to know more about it." 54 percent of the youngsters expressed the same opinion as Vimala. Only 13 percent in the age group of 31–40 and 6 percent in the age group of 41–45 said that they take initiative to express their sexual needs.

Analysis of the data discloses that women in older groups, even though they are educated and employed, still feel ashamed to take initiatives to express their sexual needs whereas women in the age group of 21–30, are found open and less inhibited on the subject of sexual matters. This probably may be due to the access to the media and the open discussions with friends that the young people have today.

Another significant finding emerged here. Although 90 percent of the Christian respondents do have access to the use of the media, still with regard to sexuality, they have not opened themselves up yet. This confirms what was said earlier about the impact of Christian teaching on sexuality.

BEAUTY AND PHYSICAL APPEARANCE

Physical beauty and appearance play a vital role in the life of a woman. Women take a lot of efforts and spend money, time and energy to make their bodies attractive and beautiful. This starts right in the early stage in the life of a female child. There is a general consensus among the respondents that early marriages are best. This finds an expression This finds an expression in a Tamil proverb which says, paruvam tavaṟiṉāl paṉaṅkiḻaṅku nārākip pōyviṭum (If the season is lost, the pulp of the palm will become fiber). It means that it is good that the girls are settled in marriage before their physical beauty fades away.

Irrespective of the group they hail from, their education, occupation, geographical location, economic position, religion and age group, 67 percent of the respondents said that physical appearance is more important than intelligence for a woman. They seem to strongly believe that physical appearance helps women to prosper in life. Moreover, it has been consistently found that women tend to focus on appearance more than men do. Often, they tend to view their bodies as objects to be seen.

According to Kamala 40, "If a woman does not marry in time, society will look down on her, especially on her parents. Moreover, today's society looks for physical appearance." The mothers who have daughters strongly opined that the girls who have a good physique will get their partners soon. Rashida Begum 29, a housewife and a Muslim said, "I have studied only up to the fifth grade. Since I took care of my physical appearance and beauty at the time of marriage I did not find it difficult to get a husband. Now, I am a wife of a business man. My husband expects me to look always appealing; so I take care of my appearance well."

For example, Ruby 29, a Christian, said:

> I work in a call centre. Often my manager makes a comment on my dress and he even fires me for not keeping myself trim and beautiful. One day he made fun of me by saying, "You are meant only to bring forth children and sing lullaby for them. Better get married and do that instead of coming here for work. Your study and intelligence are not just enough for work. You should be a smart looking woman, and it should be shown in your dress. Otherwise, better decide and get out. Today, I spend more time in beautifying myself in order to get through in life, since I am the only bread winner in my family.

Among the respondents who opined that physical appearance is more important than intelligence for a woman, 64 percent of them said that physical appearance is needed for a woman to get into a marriage market while 36 percent of them said that beauty is needed to get employment.

And the second purpose for which women care for their physical appearance is economic survival. In their struggle for survival, many women do care for their beauty, so that they could get into the job market to earn their livelihood. Irrespective of status and religion, the responses from women concerning their body and beauty care brings to light the patriarchal mandate on woman's body that makes physical beauty a necessary factor for women's survival and prosperity.

It also unveils the market logic of globalization. In the globalised market, if a woman does not bring in customers, she has not done a good job. Women are expected to bring in customers and clients and promote sales through their beauty and attractiveness. As a result, women are made to become walking embodiments of men's projected needs, reducing feminine gender identity to attractiveness to men and sexual availability on men's terms. They are to be 'businesslike yet feminine' in their appearance and approach. Ultimately it is a patriarchal legacy which uses and abuses women's beauty for its vested interest.

Beauty Care and Motivation

Amidst these oppressive and victimizing views, it is very obvious that there are women who think differently about beauty care and physical appearance. For instance Gayathri said, "I care for my body in the way I want. I do not bother to please anyone by my appearance. Especially, when my husband tells me to dress up well I simply ignore his words. Only when I feel like dressing up, I dress up well and also the way I want." In another instance, Kaanjana 42, a clerk and a mother of two children said, "In fact in my office, people tease me for being fat. But I do not bother about their comments. I do not have to reduce my body for their sake. It is my body, and I will do what I want. Who are they to construct my body?"

Catherine 40, a mother of three children and a widow said, "Since my husband is dead, society is not happy to see me dressed up well.[55] It even speaks ill of me. But I like to look nice and keep my body in a healthy and presentable manner. This I do not do for any one, but for my own satisfaction."

Among the 78 percent of the respondents who said that they care for their body, 44.6 percent of them said that they care for it in order to feel good about it. 23.4 percent of them take care of their body to please their husbands while 10 percent, to pursue a career and 12 percent, to attract others.

According to the data, occupation seems to influence the respondents' constructive motivation of beauty care. Among those who are employed, 64 percent said that they care for their body and beauty in order to feel good about themselves, while in the case of housewives, it was only 12 percent. In the same way, 78 percent of the housewives said that they dress up well in order to please their husbands while only 41 percent of those employed said so.

Analysis of the data reveals that the housewives are more concerned about pleasing their husbands even while dressing up well, whereas women who are employed are able to own their body and feel good about it. Thus, the above finding indicates that economic dependence of the housewives often deprive them autonomy and ownership over their own bodies. But economic empowerment gives women freedom to a certain extent to make decisions for their lives. Similarly, there is a close connection between the religion of the respondents and the purpose of their body and beauty care.

55. A wife becomes amaṅkali (an inauspicious woman) when her husband dies. Her body should go through a process of renunciation—a complete removal of anything that makes her body look grand and beautiful namely kuṅkumam, flowers, tāli, bangles, toe ring, anklets, silk sari etc.

Further analysis shows that there is a significant variation among the respondents based on the frequency of the use of the media. Thus the data clearly shows that respondents who are exposed to the media regularly seem to have a healthy and positive motivation for their beauty care. The media is often blamed for victimizing women to the myth of beauty. However the analysis here indicates that the media has played an affirmative role in the lives of women, enabling them to take control of their bodies.

Beauty and Color Consciousness

'Fair is beautiful and dark is ugly'. This is the slogan in the globalised market, directed to every consumer. Color consciousness is active among both men and women of Dindigul district. This is seen in the way women apply mañcaḷ[56]on their face, hands and the legs to make themselves fair. Sometimes, they go in for cosmetics available in the market in order to look fair. Their attitude towards girls who are of darker complexion also reveals the color consciousness of the respondents. They call them as kaṟuppi or karuvācci.[57] As much as possible, the mothers do not allow their daughters to go out to play. They try to apply turmeric powder to keep them looking fair. They instruct their girl children who attempt to go out to play, 'Do not play in the sun, you will become dark, No boy will marry you.'

In this context, Savariammal 40, a Christian by faith and works as a vegetable vendor in the locality said, "People say that black is beautiful, but certainly not for a girl. When a boy child is born dark, they don't make a comment, whereas when a girl child is dark, they call her by nick names like kaṟuppi or karuvācci. Women are expected to give birth to a fair baby, even if she and her husband are dark." It was also quite evident from the research area that some of the pregnant women were avoiding coffee, tea and pungent food in order to have a fair child. Women who are economically well off, take milk mixed with kuṅkumappū[58] regularly in order to make the child's skin fair.

56. Mañcaḷ is germicidal turmeric power. It is treated by many people as kirumi ṉāciṉi which means a protection from insects.

57. Kaṟuppi or karuvācci means a girl with darker complexion.

58. It is an orange—yellow spice used for flavoring and coloring food.

Lalitha 25, a post-graduate who had just celebrated the ritual of cīmantam [59]said:

> In my mother's days, people were not so much color conscious. Though my mother was dark, she could easily get married even without education. But today in spite of good education and job, women with fair complexion are preferred. Besides, those days when women were pregnant, they did not know how to go about during pregnancy except to eat good food. But today the magazines give us a lot of information about how to make our child's color fairer, what could be done to improve its health, etc. Since I am dark, my parents found it difficult to settle my marriage. I don't want my child (if it is a girl child) to go through that agony. I regularly eat kuṅkumappū [60]and avoid coffee and tea for the sake of my child's future.

It is astounding to observe from the data on the respondents' attitude towards color; a significant difference is seen among the respondents on the basis of their caste. 49 percent of BCs and 53 percent of MBCs said that they are conscious of their color, while in the case of Dalits, it was 68 percent.

Kuyili 38, a Dalit respondent said, "I usually work in my village. I do not know much about other people and places. But recently, I started going daily to Dindigul for work, due to lack of cultivation here. I see many fair women and men there. Especially, when I see fair women on the road or in the bus, I become conscious of my color." Solayee 37, a Dalit vendor said, "Whenever I watch a TV program I feel bad about my color. Especially, when I see women of fair complexion in advertisements and in other programmes, I feel inferior within me because I am dark." The study regarding color consciousness clearly confirmed the variation among the respondents of different castes.

A further scrutiny on the data on color consciousness of the respondents discloses the influence of media images on these respondents which are highly gendered. The media presentations have influenced and negatively affected the Dalit women's perceptions of themselves. Besides, it also reveals women's internalized perception which comes from a sense of rejection and shame around one's own body, especially

59. Cīmantam is a ritual performed for a pregnant woman. It is usually celebrated either at the seventh or ninth month of her pregnancy.

60. Even though so far no scientific base is available for this, women keep believing, and eat kuṅkumappū during pregnancy.

when it is dark. This is probably due to the sudden exposure to urban centers and the availability and use of the media which is a recent phenomenon among the Dalit women.

Furthermore, the broader implication was brought to the researcher's attention from the field. Women have internalized the values of society with regard to beauty. They perpetuate this beauty standard through conversations with other women by focusing on their own dissatisfaction with their color and body size or by making disparaging comments about the color or weight of others.

All the same, according to 35.6 percent of the respondents, beauty is not just being fair and slim; rather they consider beauty as being natural and capable of achieving something in life. A probe into these data discloses that there is a striking difference among the respondents based on their involvement in action-oriented groups.

To cite few examples, Muthu Lakhsmi 29, said, "I am dark. People used to tease me always with a nick name karuvācci. I used to feel bad and inferior. But after going to POORNA I began to accept my color. Slowly my understanding of beauty also has changed. Nowadays, I realize that it is not the color that makes a woman beautiful."

Chandammal 34, a member of SHG said:

> According to me, beauty does not consist in size or color of the body but in its abilities to work longer. Hence, I do not care about whether my body is fair or thin. But I am concerned about my body's abilities to co-operate with me when I work. It is work that gives me beauty. Moreover, a woman may beautify herself with artificial products but it will go away with rain or sweat or by the end of the day. But real beauty is just being natural. When the creation of a woman itself is so beautiful, why should she go in for artificial products?

According to 52 percent of the respondents who are members of action oriented groups, beauty does not go with the color or size, but rather in its ability to achieve something and also being natural. In the case of those who have no influence of these groups, only 18 percent think so.

Education does not seem to have much influence on women's understanding of beauty. Literates and illiterates are of the same view. The only variation is seen due to the impact of action-oriented groups as the above figures clearly points out.

Beauty Care and Use of Cosmetics

Women spend money to buy cosmetics to beautify themselves. They use beauty products like *Fair and Lovely, Vicco Turmeric* or *Youth Ever.* It is also noticeable that women learn about makeup and beauty care from other women, from magazines, from television ads and beauty parlors. Magazines like Kuṅkumam, Maṅkai, Kumutam, Āṉanta Vikaṭan,[61] etc., are mostly found in their homes. In Dindigul town alone there are seventy beauty parlors.[62] There are also women who give beauty care at home either for marriages or on a regular basis. Even among women from the lower middle class, the use of beauty products like *Fair and Lovely, Youth Ever, Vicco Turmeric*, etc is observable. Generally, women use make up or put mañcaḷ or facial powder while going to work and to shops, to celebrations or to the church /temple /mosque, etc.

Gowri 36, said, "My beauty is an asset for me. It brings joy and happiness for me. So, I take care of it with a best and right type of things available in the market. I always use make-up in order to look fresh and feel good about it."

Likewise Kala 37, shared, "I am only a cittāḷ. Of course, I have no money to buy costly products to appear beautiful. Still I apply mañcaḷ (Turmeric powder) and kaṭalai māvu (flour of black gram) on my face and hands in order to look beautiful." Meena 34, a flower vendor, for example, said, "Even though I am only selling flowers, still I try to keep my body neat. I bathe daily. Sometimes I apply mañcaḷ on my face and legs to protect my skin from insect bites as well as to feel good about myself."

With regard to the use of products to beautify themselves, there is a significant variation among the respondents based on their frequency of the use of the media. Among those who said that they use some products or other to look fresh, 54 percent of regular viewers of the media said that they use home-made products, whereas in the case of those who rarely view the media, it is 62 percent.

With regard to the use of beauty products, some said that they prepare on their own. Radhika, a college professor for instance, said:

61. These are Tamil secular magazines meant mostly for women.

62. This number was during the field study of the author.

> Although I watch different channels daily, still I don't rely on cosmetics that the media puts forward. Of course I have money but I am careful about the products that I use for my body. I love my body and I treasure my body. I want to give the best care for my body. So I always prepare beauty products for myself. I don't take extra time to prepare them but as I am cooking or scraping a coconut, I take a little bit of the scraped coconut, smash it and apply it on my face and hands, in order to keep my face and hands smooth. I follow lots of practical tips like this to maintain my body and beauty. I eat well and drink plenty of water. What else do you need to keep your body fresh? My body is a gift to me. When my body is in good condition, I become more active and creative.

Analysis of the above data shows that although these women are financially sound and are regular users of the media, the fact that they prepare their own beauty products discloses that they have not become victims of the media. In spite of the numerous products that the media seem to present day after day, the respondents who view the media often do not become victims of advertisements. This indicates that not all women who view the media tend to become its victims. Rather, they are able to make a healthy decision for themselves with regard to their beauty care. According to the finding, in the use of cosmetics, respondents who rarely view the media outnumber those who view the media regularly.

Besides, the data also reveals that caring for the body and its appearance, and using beauty products are seen not only among women who are economically well off but also among women in the lower rungs of society.[63] 'Caring for the body' does not mean going to beauty parlors or applying facial creams and packs, but rather caring with materials available to them within their limited resources. Such an attitude brings to light the underlying perceptions of these women who feel good and happy about their body.

BODY AND LABOR

The life of most women starts early in the wee hours of the day and ends late. Women perceive that their bodies are meant to work. They feel they are under great strain. They are not only burdened with household duties and a career, but they have also to satisfy their husbands' sexual needs.

63. In the last five years, Zaibatsu giant Hindustan Lever Ltd has released more than 250 new beauty products in India. Cf. Runkle, "The Beauty Obsession," 11.

In most of the families, the working woman rushes back home after her work outside in order to do her household chores. In the villages, while men relax after their work mostly in front of a *Panchayat* TV or at the tea shop or in a common place, women are found busy cooking, fetching water, collecting firewood, buying necessary things for the night meal, or washing the clothes of the family members, etc. As for towns and cities, usually men take a walk out after their work, or meet their friends, or watch a program on the TV, while women are found busy cooking, or teaching the children, or washing the dishes, etc.

The statistics on the respondents' perception of their work at home or outside clearly displayed that there is a significant difference between women who are employed and those remaining at home as housewives. Chitra 40, a mother of three children and a housewife said:

> My day starts at 5.00 am. From then on, I work like a machine. I prepare breakfast and lunch, get ready my children for school, keep things ready for my husband to go for work. I work the whole day cleaning, washing the clothes of my children and husband, taking care of my children's education and feeding them. Once everyone is gone to bed, then I go to bed. After a hectic day, even after going to bed I have to be on the look out to make my husband happy sexually. Otherwise I am not a good wife. After all these works, I am told by my husband cummā tānē irukkirāi (meaning you are simply sitting at home). I feel strained and bored up by the end of the day.

While sharing about their work experience, 64 percent of the housewives consider their work monotonous, burdensome and unfulfilling. Most likely, such experiences of women are due to lack of recognition of their housework as a work by society and by the family.

Considering work as a burden was found even among women who are employed. Anjamma 38, said, "I work as a cittāḷ. I find my work boring and heavy. Sometimes I do not find proper work and do not get enough wages also. Moreover, what I earn goes to my family, and I have no freedom to spend it for myself. So, I get disappointed. I do not like to go for work outside. But I have no other choices." It was not only Anjamma, but 21 percent of the respondents who had to give their entire earning to the family, expressed the same opinion. Thus, women who are employed also find their work heavy and boring, when they have no freedom to spend the money they earn.

Work as Growth

Nevertheless, not all the respondents who are employed have a negative experience of their work. 41 percent of them had a different opinion.

To cite a few examples, Radha 40, a school teacher said, "Going out for work is a joyful experience for me. Every day I see another world around me, journeying with me. Sometimes I have gained friendship with some of my co-travelers on the way to the work spot. When I realize that I am able to contribute something to society, it is so fulfilling. The day when I don't go for work I feel empty."

Kamali, a flower vendor who goes regularly to sell flowers in Madurai said, "Every day I go in the morning and return in the evening. I do not find my work a burden. I enjoy doing it. When I remained in my village, I did not know many things. By going into the city I come to know many women. I learn a lot from them. I have become very courageous also. In fact I have grown a lot"

Madhavi, a daily laborer in a local flour mill said, "I had no experience of the world outside before going for work. I was living in a small world. But after going for work, I have grown a lot in my understanding of the world and my thinking about others. I have learnt about myself also."

With regard to their perception on work, the only variation seen is due to the occupation of the respondents. Among those who are employed 72 percent of them said that they find work self-fulfilling, while in the case of housewives, it was only 36 percent.

The analysis of the above data discloses that working in two capacities, as housewives at home and wage-earners outside, either in the school or in the office or in the hospital, women's awareness of their own existence, worth and abilities has grown. Moving out also keeps them in touch with several people, thus exposing them to a whole set of new experiences. This in turn changes their views and perceptions, making them look at their surroundings in a different way.[64] This indicates how labor becomes an element of agency to give expression to one's own self. It makes women more assertive and creative. Swati Shirwadkar substantiates this from the lives of women of Marathwada in Maharastra.[65]

64. Shirwadkar, *Women and Socio-Cultural Changes*, 125–26.

65. Shirwadkar states that if a woman works outside the sphere of home, she naturally becomes capable of facing difficult and different situation. Change from a mere housewife to a woman with gainful employment widens her horizon and also leads to

Finding work as a pleasure and growth is stronger in unorganized laborers than in organized laborers. In the case of organized laborers, education and more income make them assertive. However, only 43 percent of the respondents employed in organized sectors find their work as growth and rewarding, whereas 71 percent of the respondents employed in unorganized sectors opine that they find their work as growth and satisfying.

What makes these unorganized women find their work satisfying is that 72 percent of them are responsible for their family economy.[66] Even though their earnings are meager, since they are economically independent, they are able to decide on issues that matter to them. It gives them a sense of autonomy to be able to spend for others or for themselves. It makes them feel their worth, since otherwise they are spoken of as women who are rremaining at home (cummā tānē irukkirāḷ). [67]

The participation of unorganized laborers both in the production as well as in the distribution of the produce of the field empowers them with a considerable amount of power and freedom over their social environment.

From a professional point of view, the nature of their work is such that there is more flexibility and an atmosphere of freedom in their work pattern unlike organized sectors which entails mostly discipline, regularity and monotony.

The data also shows that among those employed in unorganized sectors, 34 percent of them move into urban centers[68] regularly either in search of construction work or as itinerant vendors. Consequently, they get acquainted with new types of people every time. When a woman

---

changes in the social system. The creative skills of a person are fully utilized and the personality system attains a development. Ibid., 121.

66. The women are forced to take up the family economy in their hands because of their husbands' irresponsible behavior. Except 8 percent who are sick, 92 percent of the respondents' husbands work and earn. Among them, 17 percent indulge in extra marital affairs, while 47 percent of them return home fully drunk in the evenings after work. The money earned from the day's hard work is spent outside homes without any accountability. This type of behavior is becoming common in other parts of Tamilnadu and India too. One such example is found in the field study shared by Bisht in her article on "Women's Movement," 27.

67. Cummā tānē irukkirāḷ means that she is simply staying at home. Mostly this is said to refer to a housewife. Today many feminists raise a question with regard to this saying: Do housewives sit at home and do nothing?

68. They move to urban centers like Dindigul, Madurai, Tiruchirapalli, Karur, etc.

moves from a village to the urban centers, she finds herself in a better position to handle her body. For instance, Kannamma said, "I am a cittāḷ. I was a very shy girl. I used to be afraid of men, especially to come in front of them. Now I regularly go to work in Madurai. I have learnt a lot. Even the way I hold my body in public has changed. If someone tries to mishandle my body in the bus or in the work spot, I do not spare him." Moving into new spaces each time enables these women to expand their mental horizon as well as to discover the possibilities of their bodily abilities.[69] Thus, the expansion of physical space in this context signifies empowerment.

Work and Sexual Harassment

It was evident during the field survey that women experience physical harassments either while going for work or at their place of work. For instance Priya 32, a woman employed in a private firm said, "My manager often abuses and harasses me. But I have to earn in order to take care of my family. I have no other go. I do not like to go for work at all." 32 percent of women employed outside said that they find their work a burden due to harassment at their work-spot.

However, in situations of mishandling or maltreatment, 71 percent of the respondents employed in the unorganized sector said that they would resist the situation. In the case of the organized sector, it was only 21 percent who said that they would resist.

Thus, the analysis indicates that women employed in the unorganized sector are much more assertive in exercising their autonomy than women employed in the organized sector. This may probably be because of the pattern of work in which that the unorganized women are involved.

A constant exposure to sun, rain, heat, cold, unsafe forests, fields, and hills and exposure to hard work have made these unorganized women of Dindigul district physically and psychologically strong and brave. Their power to face any hardship and danger—not as stereotyped victims but as agents—is something unique. It is this power that Sen and Batliwala would name as 'power to.'[70]

69. Rao, *Women and Society*, 71.

70. Malhotra et al., "Measuring Women's Empowerment," 2.

In addition, whether in the field or in the market or in the construction spot, working and interacting with different men is the common experience of most women employed in unorganized sectors. This provides them with opportunity to have a better understanding of males, removing from their minds the patriarchal stereotype that *men are superior and strong*. Women deal with men as one among them, not considering them higher, even in the way they address them. Hitting back when men try to abuse them is clearly an indication of women's agency.

Conclusion

To sum up, an in-depth exploration into the socio-cultural perceptions of women from Dindigul district with regard to their bodies discloses that not all the respondents of our present study are victims of a given situation. However, the data does disclose a sense of fear, shame and kuṭumpa kauravam attached to the women's understanding of their body, motherhood, dress code, space, menstruation, beauty and sexuality.

Running through their stories are also tales of consciousness, agency and resistance. They are not merely acted upon, nor are they merely powerless pawns embedded in the discursive struggles that determine existence. They show their resistance to the destructive and alienating discourses associated with the female body. The statistical analysis on the data reveals that the factors like exposure to urban life, media, involvement in action-oriented groups, higher education and employment act as tools of empowerment. They place women in a better position to exercise autonomy and to take control of their body.

Deeper analysis also shows the complex nature in the self-perceptions of respondents who are economically well-off. Respondents who are unexposed to the outside world tend to hold on to a conventional ideology of body while those exposed to urban centers are able to go beyond the patriarchal conditionings. All the same, when it comes to preoccupation with kuṭumpa kauravam, respondents who are economically well-off score the highest. This exposes the deep-rooted traditional attitude in those who are exposed to the outside world as well.

Another significant finding of this research is that the respondents employed in the unorganized sector are much more assertive in exercising their autonomy than women employed in the organized sector. All the same what emerges remarkably from the data is that when it is a matter of survival, irrespective of the religion, caste, social and economic status, educational qualification, and the geographical location, women do not hesitate to throw away the existing socio-cultural and religious perceptions of their body. Following Butler,[71] I argue that woman's body is in a process of becoming. As an ongoing discursive practice, it is open to intervention and resignification. What this would imply is a view of female agency as, at once, rooted in bodily identity and also engaging with a socio-spatial order that constitutes and defines it.

Having analyzed the qualitative data of the respondents of the present study to identify the elements of agency in their self-perceptions, the next chapter moves on to argue hermeneutically that the reclaiming of women's bodies is disclosed in these elements of agency.

71. Butler, *Gender Trouble*, 33.

4

Reclaiming the Body, Beauty, and Sexuality

An in-depth exploration into the socio-cultural perceptions of women from Dindigul district has brought into relief some of the underlying perceptions surrounding their body. While a vast majority is found victims of the existing situation, a small segment of women has begun to exercise their bodily agency. The findings lucidly reveal *many faces of women's agency* at work. Despite the patriarchal norms that remain deeply embedded in the social and economic structures of Tamil society, there are some who have begun to resist,[1] move beyond and create a space for themselves. They have not only moved out of their private space to public space but also have begun to redefine their identities beyond those of daughter, wife and mother. They deconstruct and reconstruct their body-space, the myth of motherhood and beauty, marriage and sexuality as a tool of identity assertion and as a mode of their quest for self-expression. This indicates that change of perception is at work in these women because of the *new consciousness* of themselves. As we already made a note in the clarification of the term *perception,* change of self-perception is possible, when the *new consciousness* takes hold of a person. However, the book does not attempt to say that the situation of women has completely changed. This finding has proved the hypothesis of the research that was made in the introduction.

1. While writing about the resistance of peasants, James C. Scott in his *Weapons of the Weak* says, "It is precisely the fusion of self-interest and resistance that is the vital force animating the resistance of peasants and proletarians. When a peasant hides part of his crop to avoid paying taxes, he is both filling his stomach and depriving the state of grain." Cf. Scott, *The Weapon of the Weak*, 295. Such resistance is not the monopoly of lower classes. Tax evasion and black economy in advanced capitalist countries are also forms of resistance, pursued with vigour and success by middle and upper classes.

Having proved the hypothesis, this chapter attempts to hermeneutically interpret further the meaning of *agency* found in the women respondents of Dindigul district, taking into consideration their patriarchal context. From a broad framework of contemporary feminism and using concepts, arguments and insights from Indian and Western feminists, this chapter also argues that *agency* acts as a key and matrix of this border-crossing and that reclaiming of women's bodies is disclosed in these elements of *agency.*

THE UNCONVENTIONAL WOMAN AND FEMINISM

From now on, the respondents who exercised *agency* are referred to as *the unconventional women.*[2] The concept of *unconventional women* is derived from the notion of new women which is located specifically within the experience of feminism. In Western literature, women started to move out of their invisibility and silence in the 19th century when Ibsen's Nora in *A Doll's House* provided a model of the new woman by saying "no" to the male power structure. Feminist scholars contend that one of the major objectives of women's liberation movements "has been to free women from the cultural demand for self-effacement and to establish their right to full human development."[3]

The term 'unconventional woman' in this book means, a woman, who, instead of imitating men, tries to actualize her authentic self; attempts to evolve a pattern of her own thinking-process, and does not blindly toe the line set for her by the male-dominated order; rejects all social and cultural images; crosses the cultural norms of femininity and empowers herself. A woman is 'unconventional' if her basic concerns are deeper than merely seeking equality with men, asserting her own personality and insisting upon her own rights as a woman.[4] In one sense, she is a rebel, but she is also conscious of herself as a 'being.' She is aware of her strength as a female individual. Indeed, she is a woman in the entire social pattern, moral code and spiritual realm.[5]

2. Although the unconventional women identified by the author are only minorities among the respondents, still they are very important for our study because they exercise *agency.*

3. Paris, *Imagined Human Beings*, 39.

4. Srivastava, *The New Woman*, 18.

5. Bande and Atma, *Woman in Indian Short Stories*, 146.

The unconventional woman is an individual with the capacity to reflect on her own position and speak for herself. She not only has economic independence, but also psychological strength to stand on her own.[6] The unconventional woman is in fact, the "female hero"[7] free to make her choices and accept self-responsibility. When a woman is able to deconstruct her dependence syndrome and counter the conditions that devalue her, she achieves the essential consciousness of herself as *a subject*, rather than as an object, sees her whole being as an agent rather than as a victim.

RECLAIMING THE BODY

"This Body is mine and Nobody's," "I do not want to end my life just in bringing forth children," "I want to care for my body," "I feel good about my body," these oft repeated phrases of the unconventional women of Dindigul district lucidly unveil their desire to take control of their bodies.

Reclaiming one's own body is the most prominent impetus of the unconventional women who exercise agency at different phases of their life. It can be argued that under the impact of feminism and feminist movements, women all over are beginning to exercise autonomy over themselves. However, how the unconventional women of Dindigul district exercise autonomy to reclaim their bodies is the query we pose at this juncture.

For the women, the particular patriarchal context in which they live and move about, reclaiming their bodies is often a difficult process because the construction of the body is embedded in a larger social framework of patriarchy.

The author focuses on the motherhood, marriage, sexuality and beauty in which women were found to exercise agency strongly in order to reclaim their bodies. The identified elements of agency are dealt with and presented under separate titles, namely, 'Body as Agency,' 'Sexuality as Agency' and 'Beauty as Agency.' Moreover, the independent self must be understood as a consequence of a social environment, because a person's conception or perception of the body is strongly directed and shaped by the culture in which one is living as well as by the relations with others in their socio-cultural context. Hence, socio-cultural contexts are taken into consideration while interpreting the meaning of *women's agency* from the field.

6. Ibid., 146–47.

7. This term is taken from Westkott, *The Feminist Legacy*, 199–214.

BODY AS AGENCY

Under 'body as agency' one of the significant findings from the field which manifest women's agency is discussed, namely how the unconventional women deconstruct the myth of motherhood to reclaim their bodies.

Motherhood as a Social Construct

Motherhood is a universal phenomenon that is simultaneously biological and social. Many women have been honored as ammā in the political, spiritual and religious pantheon. Nevertheless, a woman who has fulfilled her simple, traditional role of a "mother" has embodied her highest office in Tamil society.

In Tamil patriarchal society, the female body has been constructed around the status of motherhood. There is so much in Tamil literature that upholds the role of motherhood. Starting from Tolkāppiyam and Tirukkuṟaḷ to Tiruvācakam, motherhood is given the highest position. As a mother, the status accorded to a woman is parallel to none other. There are so many lyrics composed to highlight the importance of mother. The phrase tāimaiyē peṇmai meaning motherhood is womanhood brings to light the importance attached in Tamil culture to a woman when she becomes a mother.

Be it in the arts, literature or movies, mother has been venerated precisely because of her capability of giving life, her fertility.[8] The Indus valley terracotta portrays women with full-breasts and wide hips which symbolize the role of "abundance" of a mother, because women are socialized as 'breeders' and 'caretakers.'[9]

Even a contemporary Tamil poet Abdul Rahman's statement about motherhood confirms this. He writes, "A woman becomes a woman when she becomes a mother."[10] In the same way, Packia Raj, a well-known Tamil film director, says, "At the time of birth, a woman is 25 percent a woman; at the time of puberty, she is 50 percent a woman; at the time of marriage she is 75 percent a woman; and at the time of child-birth she becomes a complete woman."[11] This was echoed in the following state-

8. Doshi, "Myth of Motherhood," 4.

9. Cf. Campbell, ed. *Myths and Symbols.*

10. As quoted by Padmavathi, Peṇ Moḻi (The Language of a Woman), 19.

11. As cited in Thilkavathi, IPS, Cinimāvukku Cila Kēḷvikaḷ (Some Questions to

ment of one of the respondents:[12] "Whoever it may be, a woman must bring forth a child. Then only she is complete." Thus motherhood is seen as the fullness of womanhood reducing her to her reproductive ability.

Radha S. Hegde writes, "Traditional images of motherhood and the ideal woman continue to shape and circumscribe women's roles in contemporary Indian society."[13]

Adrienne Rich makes a similar comment. She writes, "Woman's status as child-bearer having 'been made into a major fact of her life and terms like 'barren" or "childless" serving as markers of negation with no male analogue like "non-father"; the bodies of women become sites for hi-tech reproductive technology."[14] She concludes, "the patriarchal institution of motherhood is not the "human condition" any more than rape, prostitution and slavery are."[15] The idealization of women as mothers, the romanticization of motherhood and the attribution of normative quality to motherhood are seen as dictated by patriarchal power relations. Anything that disrupts this power relationship such as illegitimacy, abortion or lesbianism is considered deviant or criminal.[16]

Rajam Krishnan, one of the Tamil feminists observes aptly, "In Tamil society a woman may be doing wonderful things in life but if she fails to be a good mother, her life is a failure. First she needs to be a mother and then everything else."[17] In spite of its noble status, the myth of motherhood is tied to the dignity and worth of the female body.

Conboy observes rightly the plight of woman in the name of motherhood. She states, "For woman, this entrapment of motherhood is particularly centered in the biological processes of childbirth that have delineated her productivity and circumscribed her movements."[18] Thus motherhood is considered as the anchor of womanhood in Tamil soci-

---

Cinema), 16.

12. In personal communication with a respondent.

13. Hegde, "Sons and Mothers," 25.

14. Rich, *Of Woman Born*, 11.

15. Ibid., 33.

16. Ibid., 42.

17. Krishnan, Kālam Tōrum Peṇmai (Women Through the Years), 44. This was also observed by Kalpana Ram in her book on Tamil women. She writes how female identity and subjectivity are firmly anchored in the tasks of social reproduction performed as mothers. Cf. Ram, *Mukkuvar Women*, 49.

18. Conboy *Writing on the Body*, 2; cf. also Kaplan and Rogers, "The Definition of Male and Female."

ety. Motherhood and femininity are significant concepts, and they are often inter-linked with each other and equated.

In such a context, where reproduction is essentialized and female body is made significant only by its exercise or role of motherhood, the unconventional women dare to deconstruct the myth of motherhood by refusing to be mere vessels that carry children, by reclaiming their womb and by relocating the barren bodies.

Deconstructing the Myth of Motherhood

Ashley Montagu defines the *myth of motherhood* as, "women getting married, bringing forth children, staying at home to nurse and care for their children, preparing meals, and performing virtually all other domestic duties."[19]

The phrases we heard from some of the women from Dindigul district such as "I do not want to end my life just being a mother," "I do not have to prove to the world my fertility," clearly manifest women's autonomy over their womb and body. In a context where a woman is made to find fulfillment only in motherhood and the productivity of a woman's body lies in her ability to bring forth children, such statements clearly manifest that these women do not want to reduce their bodies to mere vessels that carry only children and to accept passively what the society expects them to be. This not only challenges society's power and hold over their body but also underscores women's redefinition of their identity. Although society treats motherhood as one of the great achievements of woman, women themselves do not see it that way. Rather they see their body beyond simple procreation. By this they not only contest and trespass the social boundaries as traditional mothers but also deconstruct the stereotypes and the naturalistic view of their bodies.

To reject society's power over their bodies, women exercise their "power from within" which Seemanthini defines as agency.[20] Sarah Lucia Hoagland also makes a similar observation. She understands "power-from-within" as "the power of ability, of choice and engagement. It is creative; and hence it is an affecting and transforming power but not

19. Cf. Montagu, *The Natural Superiority of Women*, 67–68.

20. Niranjana, *Gender and Space*, 34.

a controlling power."[21] This is the power that unconventional women exercise to reclaim their bodies.

Beyond Simple Procreation

Another significant way the unconventional women reclaim their bodies is through their contribution which goes beyond simple procreation. The phrase "My body is also capable of achieving many more things in life" brings to light the consciousness and assertion of their bodily abilities which are far greater than just giving birth and restricting their role as mothers.

Feminism, since the publication in 1792 of Mary Wollstonecraft's *Vindication of the Rights of Woman*, has always been concerned with the relation of women to their bodies—wombs in particular. That relation is seen as an oppressive one: biology is destiny; women's work is reproduction, not production; the womb is the site of hysteria; and woman equals immanence while man equals transcendence.

A feminist reclaiming of the body and in particular the mother's womb begins fittingly with homage to Simone de Beauvoir. According to de Beauvoir, Feminism advocates freedom and autonomy, via a flight from body. The body is understood as a shackle, a chain to be freed from. It limits freedom by its materiality, corporeality and its being *given*. More importantly, the body has been understood as a justification of the naturalness of sexual division of labor, which in turn, gives credence to the productive/ reproductive labor divide. Thus, to be identified with reproductivity (menstruation, pregnancy, lactation), a woman sets herself up to continuing oppression and otherness.[22]

Unlike Beauvoir, some of the feminists like Betty Friedan and Nancy Hartsock had different opinions regarding motherhood. For example, in 1981, Betty Friedan brought out her *The Second Stage23* with its emphasis on the women's need to cherish the human labor of nurture and the security of close relationships. She argues that "there is a power in women's ability to create life, closeness to life that men don't have."[24] Virginia Held views women's unique experiences as mothers and

21. Hoagland, *Lesbian Ethics*, 118.

22. Beauvoir, *The Second Sex*, 152; Cf. Brike, L. *Women, Feminism and Biology.*

23. See Friedan, *The Second Stage.*

24. Ibid., 161.

caregivers as the basis for new insights into power. As she puts it, "the capacity to give birth and to nurture and empower could be the basis for new and more humanly promising conceptions than the ones that now prevail of power, empowerment, and growth."[25]

Nancy Hartsock said, "The experience of menstruation, coitus, pregnancy and lactation, which challenged body boundaries, gives women a greater experience of continuity with nature already lost by men. Women's labor in caring for men and children and producing basic values in the home, gives them more rootedness and a more basic understanding of life processes than men."[26] Thus while the early radical feminists denied the bodily reality of women and fostered patriarchal alienation from the body,[27] later radical feminists on the other hand, moved from seeing women's biology as the problem to women's biology as the solution. They affirm their potentialities to become mothers.

A closer look at the perceptions of unconventional women concerning motherhood shows that they do not completely reject the state of motherhood; rather they oppose the attitude of essentializing motherhood for women. In philosophical circles, essentialism refers to the belief that things have essences, understood as fixed properties that define and limit what a thing is, sharply delineating it from what it is not. Essentialist arguments often emerge in discussions of categories such as race, gender and sexuality.[28] In an essentialist position, these categories are fixed, determined, and/ or grounded on real essential features of an individual's biology or psychology.[29]

Sociologists like Thomas Laqueur,[30] Duroche,[31] and Ludmilla Jordanova,[32] speak of biological reductionism[33] of woman to her body. In contrast to the above notion that biology determines the destiny of women, the unconventional women of the present study cry out for

25. Held, *Feminist Morality*, 137.

26. Hartsock, *Money, Sex, and Power*, 54.

27. Saivings, "Human Situation," 19–32.

28. Plaskow, "Embodiment and Ambivalence," 33.

29. http://mingo.info-science.uiowa.edu/stevens/critped/terms.htm)—Accessed on 23rd of July 2006.

30. Laqueur, "Orgasm, Generation,"; idem, *Making Sex: Body and Gender.*

31. Duroche, "Male Perception as a Social Construct."

32 Jordanova, *Sexual Visions.*

33. Fausto-Sterling, *Myths of Gender*, 11–3; also Bleier, *Science and Gender.*

exercise and for the discipline of applying their mind to some useful purpose outside the home. A woman is more than a producer of an off-spring. This in itself is a radical progression from the older world-view, which sees them as irrevocably doomed. The unconventional women's perception of their body beyond procreation challenge the age-old notion of motherhood. This affects the definition of a 'normal' woman, a woman who will protect the patriarchal social order.[34] However, this stance is neither meant to trivialize nor negate the body's importance; rather it is meant to call attention to the reality that no matter how low or poor or illiterate, rich or beautiful, the woman is all the time justifying her existence as a woman and her right to a personally perceived meaningful life.

It is in place to recall here what Tishani Doshi writes about the empowerment of women's bodies. She puts it aptly, "Only when a woman is empowered with her own reproductive rights, when she is emancipated from the various myths that surround her, when she has the freedom to explore the full range of her abilities and energies, will she realize what is feminine, what is mother, what is beyond simple procreation."[35]

Relocating the 'Issueless' Bodies

Another significant way through which the unconventional women deconstruct the myth of motherhood is by relocating the issueless body back into society.

For centuries, the Tamil society honors a married woman with the status of cumaṅkali, only when she gives birth to a child, preferably a male child. "Having a child is highly creative both in the physical sense of producing it and in the social sense of molding it." She gets the honor of being present as well as to perform ceremonies especially at the time of a wedding, cīmantam, puberty rite, and at any auspicious event that takes place at home. But an infertile body has to live with a stigma of being barren. A barren woman is considered inauspicious at all social and religious functions. "Better to be mud than a barren woman" goes one of the Tamil proverbs.[36] Besides, in the shame and suffering of being

34. Game, *Undoing the Social.*

35. Doshi, "Myth of Motherhood," 4.

36. Bande says that barrenness as a curse is depicted in many Indian short stories and novels. Cf. Bande, *Woman in Indian Short Stories*, 75.

the "unproductive" maternal body, there are dominant discourses which intersect the everyday practices of these women.

Sociological studies in India show that childlessness is one of the potent causes of domestic violence against women. They suffer in multiple ways: stigma of being barren, the resultant loneliness, and taunts by the husband and his family.[37] "He beats me heartlessly every evening for minor lapses and sometimes for no reason at all," said one of the respondents who has no issue.[38] Thus the barren women are not only denied public space but also become victims of domestic violence.[39]

While making an observation on the plight of barren women in Tamil Society, Radha S. Hegde states, "These are expressions of a systematic rearticulation of patriarchal ideologies that ensure the dependence and vulnerability of women."[40] Similarly Uma Shankar Jha and Others aptly illustrate, "Whether she is poor or wealthy, high or low, an Indian woman knows that motherhood confers upon her a purpose and identity that nothing else in her culture can."[41]

Against this background, the unconventional women dare to raise questions such as "What is there to feel bad about?" "If one of our organs is defective and does not function well, will we curse the body?" These questions externally seem to dilute the significance of the function of a woman's womb. But in a given context where the dignity and honor of a woman is dependent on the fertility of her womb, relocating these women who have infertile wombs, back into their respective societies becomes highly significant.

This changing attitude of unconventional women contravenes religious and cultural teaching and outlook towards barren body which equates the failure of one organ with the whole body, labeling it and treating it as a curse; making one to live constantly with guilt and shame; and hampering it from social and religious participation. In a special way, this defies not only the conventional blessings showered upon ev-

37. For further details refer Kudchedkar and Sabiha, ed., *Violence against Women.*

38. In personal communication with her at Kosava Patti, Dindigul District—02.04.04.

39. Arundati Roy also in her book speaks about the violence done to barren women among Syrian Christian community. Cf. *The God of Small Things*, 47–8.

40. Hegde, "Sons and Mothers," 26.

41. Shankar Jha et al., *Status of Indian Women—Volume 2.*

ery bride on the day of the wedding[42] but also the sacred scriptures and literature, which uphold motherhood as the highest role for a woman.

What is striking is that by daring to break the stereotypes pertaining to issueless women and asserting their claim over their bodies, the unconventional women not only confront society's claim over their bodies but also deconstruct the sacred ceremonies like pūppuṉita nīrāṭṭu viḻā, cīmantam, marriage, etc in which hitherto only auspicious women could take part. This brings into focus the question of the divide between the auspicious and the inauspicious body.

"One of the devices of patriarchy is to divide and rule and to treat one as superior over the other, namely pure/impure, male/female, and sacred/profane," writes Chris Shilling.[43] Patriarchy divides women's bodies into auspicious and inauspicious. The inauspicious women are more marginalized and confined to a certain space.

Issueless women who are socialized in such societies, internalize these myths, and could develop a negative valuation of their bodies and thus consider themselves as having less capability, dignity and honor as compared to women who are fertile. In their wretched state of life, when issueless women are allowed to take part in the sacred rituals and ceremonies, it is a time once again to make them feel assured of their self-worth and dignity. One could even argue that one's sense of self-worth should not depend on the participation in these ceremonies and rituals.

In Tamil society, performance of these rituals functions as a powerful means not only in the shaping of the social ethos, but also in the articulation, redefinition and legitimating of cultural realities.[44] The studies of Foucault[45] and Bourdieu[46] show that ritual action plays a significant role in the construction of the social body. For Foucault, ritual is the social construction of a body by which "the person" is afforded a particular sense of identity vis-à-vis other groups in which power is localized. This construction of identity simultaneously empowers the person as well as limits or constricts the person.[47] For issueless women who are denied such participation and performance in rituals, taking

42. Bumiller, *May You Be the Mother*, 101–24.

43. Shilling, *The Body*, 15.

44. Bell, *Ritual Theory*, 299.

45. Michel Foucault, *Discipline and Punish*.

46. Cf. Bourdieu, *Outline of a Theory of Practice*.

47. Bell, *Ritual Theory*, 308–9.

part in these ceremonies do matter a lot to regain their self-worth. It symbolically frees them from guilt and shame and affirms and empowers them to live with dignity and honor.

Moreover, this daring act in fact defiles the sacredness of the rituals and bulldozes the patriarchal mechanisms to control women. Thus the unconventional women are able to make real the fact that human beings are more important than ceremonies and rituals. This clearly manifests women's insistence not only on a reassessment of their social function but also on being valued as individuals functioning creatively and productively within society instead of being simply looked at as wives, mothers, daughters and caretakers.

Thus a new definition of the woman's body emerges. This new definition of a woman is not restricted to mere reproductive functions but goes beyond that. In this definition, women do not structure their world around the so-called feminine ideologies.

BEAUTY AS AGENCY

Beauty care and physical appearance remain vital factors in most of the women respondents whom I interviewed. It is obvious even among the women who work in unorganized sectors.[48] But what constitutes beauty and physical appearance varies from one woman to another.

Apparently, the unconventional women's perception of beauty and physical appearance disclose elements of empowerment and autonomy. I explore under 'Beauty as Agency' how the unconventional women reclaim their bodies through their perception of beauty care in the given patriarchal context where female beauty is often constructed and determined.

Redefining Female Beauty

The concept of female beauty differs from place to place, and culture to culture. Feminist anthropology shows that people experience and understand their body and beauty according to a culturally defined image. There is no objective physical body that is perceived in the same way by all cultures. Bodies and body parts are loaded with cultural symbolism.[49]

48. 42 percent of the respondents who work in unorganized sectors opined that beauty and physical appearance are important for them.

49. Synnott, *The Body Social*, 1.

Besides, terms such as *fat*, *old*, *beautiful*, *strong*, and *handsome* are defined within particular cultural contexts. Each language encodes a set of culturally relative premises about ideals. A vivid example of the culturally specific dimension of beauty is provided by Estes,[50] who describes the mismeasuring of children according to a particular body ideal accepted in the United States.

Tamil culture too has made female beauty an attractive factor. Most of Tamil literature emphasizes only the physical beauty and appearance of women. The description of a woman's bodily organs gets prime importance in poems, songs and arts that portray women. In a way, the beauty myth is not something new to Tamil culture and society. It is as old as terracotta. Physical beauty not only plays a vital role but also a determining factor in the life of a woman, especially at the time of marriage.

In such a context where female beauty is defined by society, the unconventional women of Dindigul district exercise agency to redefine their perception and treatment of beauty in the following ways.

Beauty as Self-Assertion

Female beauty has always been the domain of men. The Tamil culture too treats the female body and beauty as the possession of her husband. The myth of Kāraikālammayār (the lady of Karaikal) illustrates beautifully the notion that the beauty of the wife is meant for her husband alone. The myth goes like this.

> One day the merchant Paramatattan was given two mangoes as a gift. He handed them over to his wife Punithavathiyar, and she gave one of them to a devotee of Siva who begged for food. She served the other to her husband during his meal, and he so liked

50. In her book, Estes writes about her Opalanga who was mocked for being too tall and thin, with a gap in her front teeth. Later Estes herself was criticized for being short and fat, which was interpreted as a sign of her inferiority and lack of self-control. But when each of these women travelled back to the land of their ancestors, each found many people who looked just like them. Opalanga journeyed to Gambia in West Africa, where many people are tall and slender like yew trees. They call the split between their front teeth *Sakaya Yallah*, or "opening of God," and interpret a space between the teeth as a sign of wisdom. When Estes travelled to the coast of Oaxaca, in Southeastern Mexico, she met "giant women who were strong and commanding in their size. They had patted me and plucked at me, boldly remarking that I was not quite fat enough. Did I eat enough? Had I been ill? I must try harder, they explained, for women are *La Tierra*, made round like the earth herself, for the earth holds so much." Cf. Estes, *Women Who Run*, 201–2.

> the taste that he asked for the other. In desperation the wife appealed to Siva, and another mango appeared in her hand. When she served this to her husband, he immediately detected the divine flavor and asked his wife where she had obtained the fruit. She told him the truth. "If that is how it happened, bring me yet another fruit," he said. She went away and prayed to god, "If you do not give me another, my word will appear false," and immediately another mango appeared. She gave this to her husband, and as he took it, it vanished. In terror at this demonstration of sacred power, Paramatattan fled across the seas to another land. Eventually he returned to dwell in the Pandiya land. He took another wife and fathered a daughter, whom he named after his first wife.
>
> However, when relatives of his learned of his presence there, they brought Punithavathiyar to him in a litter. He fell at her feet and worshipped her. At this the relatives were shocked and ashamed. "Is it right for you to worship your own wife?" they cried. "She is not a woman but a goddess," answered the merchant. And he said "As soon as I discovered this, I left her; now I have married a real woman and called my daughter by the name of my former wife, our family deity." Hearing these words, Punithavathiyar prayed to Siva, "Until now I have carried this bag of flesh for the sake of my husband. If this is how he feels, I no longer need this body of mine which is not useful for him; give me the form of a demon (Pēy vativu) who worships your feet." Siva dried up her flesh, and she became a demoness roaming the forest of Alankadu. In the final apotheosis, the devoted wife sacrifices her body and its beauty. Kāraikālammayār, a woman noted for her beauty and prettiness, takes up an ugly form, just because the husband does not use it.[51]

Thus the female body is meant for a man. If the husband is not able to enjoy it, then there is no use of its existence. Hence it has to be destroyed. Sati is probably the aftermath of this kind of myth. Wives especially are expected to look beautiful and auspicious to please the gaze of their husbands.

The patriarchal practice of making an exhibition of woman's beauty is seen not only at the beauty contest conducted by the commercial markets, but also in every house in the form of peṇ pārkkum paṭalam (the ceremony of visiting the bride-to-be).

51. Shulman, *Tamil Temple Myths*, 34.

Simone de Beauvoir rightly observes, "In the regime of institutionalized heterosexuality, a woman must make her body and beauty an object and prey for the man: it is for him that these eyes are limpid pools, this cheek baby-smooth."[52] Bartky says, 'In contemporary patriarchal culture, a panoptical male connoisseur resides within the consciousness of most women. They stand perpetually before his gaze and under his judgment. A woman lives her body as seen by another, an anonymous patriarchal *other*.'[53]

Simone de Beauvoir speaks of patriarchy as characterized by women's internalization of otherness[54], and Berger speaks about the "male gaze," which leads to women's objectification.[55] Above all, no matter how assertive she may be in the world, a woman's private submission to the control of her husband is what makes her desirable and beautiful.

Yet the oft repeated phrases of the unconventional women of the present study, 'To feel good about myself,' and 'I dress up the way I want' bring out their assertive attitude towards beauty and physical appearance. The statement of one of the unconventional women confirmed this, "I do not care what others think of me. I live the way I want, and I dress up the way I want." Such an assertion deconstructs the myth that women are to please men with their appearance,[56] so that culture can be kept male.

Feeling good about oneself is closely linked to a sense of pride about oneself. A person is proud about oneself for various reasons. It can be for internal or external reasons or for both. Psychologists are of the opinion that the external reasons for one to feel proud about oneself can come when someone achieves something in life, or is given a public applause or status in society. On the other hand, the internal reason for one to feel proud about oneself can arise when someone accepts oneself or when one realizes that he or she is the master or owner of his/her life. Ownership implies freedom, autonomy and possession. In this book, ownership means women taking or having control over the situation, with regard to their bodies. This ownership also leads one to self-assertion and affirmation, either privately or publicly.

52. For more information, see Beauvoir, *The Second Sex*, 642.
53. As cited in Jackson et al. *Women Studies: A Reader*, 228.
54. Beauvoir, *The Second Sex*, 529.
55. Cf. Berger, *Ways of Seeing*.
56. Young, "Racializing Femininity," 67–86.

Ultimately, choosing to look how and what they want to be, unveils women's exercise of agency. What underlies their perception is reclamation of their body.

This is in conformity with what Natalie Beausoliel writes, "When women orient their appearance practices to their partners or outside audiences or the public they seem to become victims of the beauty myth. On the other hand, when they orient their appearance practices to feel good about themselves and for one's own satisfaction, they become agents of their own."[57]

Magtoto rightly observes, "A body that is scarred, used and discarded is a body you don't feel your own. But the process of coming to terms with it awakens in you the desire to care for it and to own it, defying anyone who thinks that they can destroy it and therefore destroy you."[58] While speaking about human agency, Goffman says that this acceptance of self is vital to a person's self-identity as a competent and worthwhile human being.[59]

Thus the women of the present study turn their beauty into a source of power for themselves by constructing their body-beauty as a tool of identity assertion and as a mode of their quest for self-expression. Ultimately, a feminist reclaiming of body and beauty begins with feeling good about one's own body.

Rejection of Conventional Media Image of Beauty

The global media has been playing a decisive role in imaging and perpetuating the ideal of female beauty. Urban India's middle and upper class women have experienced a veritable revolution in commercial beauty products and beauty culture since the economic liberalization in 1991.[60] Every other week, a new issue of *Femina, Woman's Era61* and other women's magazines appear in the book-stalls, instructing women how to appear better and smarter. The patriarchal practice of making an exhibition of woman's beauty is seen not only at the beauty contest conducted by the commercial markets, but also in every house in the form of peṇ pārkkum paṭalam (the ceremony of visiting the bride – to – be).

57. Beausoliel, "Makeup in Everyday Life," 33.
58. Magtoto, L. C. *Birthings: A Journal of Shared Lives*, 21.
59. As cited in Shilling, *The Body*, 85.
60. Runkle, "The Beauty Obsession," 11.
61. These are English magazines mostly published for women in India.

Women's beauty is portrayed as an object of attraction, whether it is on the television or on the wall posters or in the pages of magazines. The advertising companies not only make use of them as objects for a good sale but they also impose certain standards of beauty on these women.

Concerns about the way women are made to perceive their bodies have risen in recent years as rates of eating disorders such as anorexia have increased, particularly among young women. Under the impact of the media they are made to feel insecure with their body- size and color. Dieting is one discipline imposed upon a female body subject to the 'tyranny of slenderness"[62]; exercise is another. Women's magazines that publish articles on dieting and fat burning exercises are increasing. 'Fat is out and thin is in' is the mantra ruling the fashion world. Moreover, thinness and fairness are promoted as essential criteria of beauty.[63]

The answer of the one of the respondents in this context is revealing. "When I watch girls on the TV channels, I hate my color and appearance. I started to buy cosmetics to improve my appearance."[64]

This corroborates what Sociologist Deborah L. Sheppard described in *The Sexuality of Organization*, "The informal rules and guidelines about the appropriateness of appearance keep shifting, which helps explain the continuous appearance of books and magazines which tell women how to look and behave at work."[65] Media activist Jean Kilbourne concludes that, "Women are sold to the diet industry by the magazines we read and the television programs we watch, almost all of which make us feel anxious about our weight."[66]

Katie says:

> Under the current "tyranny of slenderness", women are forbidden to become large or massive; they must take up as little space as possible. The very contours a woman's body takes on as she matures- the fuller breasts and round hips- have become distasteful. The body by which a woman feels herself judged and which by

62. Phrase taken from the title of Kim Chernin's *The Obsession*.

63. The same issue is discussed in the following article too. Bond and T. Cash "Black Beauty," 874–88.

64. In personal communication with her at Dindigul—24.01.04.

65. As cited in Wolf, *The Beauty Myth*, 42.

66. Gerber, "Beauty and Body Image in the Media," Online: www.media-awarenes sca/english/issues /stereotyping/women_and_girls/women_beauty.cfm , 1. Accessed on 11.09.2005; Cf. also George D. "Medical Complications of Anorexia," 22–32; Bordo, "Reading the Slender Body."

> rigorous discipline she must try to assume is the body of early adolescence, slight and unformed—a body lacking flesh or substance, a body in whose very contours the image of immaturity has been inscribed. The requirement that a woman maintain a smooth and soft skin carries further the theme of inexperience, for an infantilised face must accompany her infantilised body, a face that never ages or furrows its brow in thought. The face of the ideally feminine woman must never display the marks of character, wisdom, and experience that we so admire in men.[67]
>
> Thus the beauty myth of the present is more insidious than any mystique of femininity. It destroys women physically and depletes them psychologically. And female beauty has been commercialized systematically.[68]

Feminists have varied opinions regarding women who use beauty products. While writing about the impact of the beauty myth on the lives of American women, Naomi Wolf states:

> As women released themselves from the feminine mystique of domesticity, the beauty myth took over its lost ground, expanding as it waned to carry on its work of social control. The beauty myth has grown stronger to take over the work of social coercion those myths about motherhood, domesticity, chastity, and passivity, no longer can manage. It is seeking right now to undo psychologically and covertly all the good things that feminism did for women materially and overtly.[69]

In the same way, Germaine Greer describes a western woman who has fallen victim to a beauty myth "a Stereotype": "To her belongs all that is beautiful, even the very word beauty itself . . . . She is a doll . . . I'm sick of the masquerade."[70] In 1962, Betty Friedan lamented that in the past, "there was no other way for a woman to be a heroine" than to "keep on having babies"; today, a heroine must "keep on being beautiful."[71] Annette Kuhn says, "The beauty myth has simply taken over the func-

67. Katie, *Writing on the Body*, 141; Cf. also Brook, *Feminist Perspectives on the Body*; Orbach, *Fat is a Feminist issue.*

68. Cf. also Featherstone, *The Dialectic of Sex*; Wolf, *The Beauty Myth.*

69. Wolf, *The Beauty Myth*, 11.

70. Ibid., 12.

71. Ibid., 66–7.

tion of Friedan's "religion" of domesticity. The terms have changed but the effect is the same."[72]

Amidst these voices of Western women, the oft repeated statements of the unconventional women like "I want to take care of my body with the right type of things available; I make my own products, I go by what convinces me," disclose convincingly that they do not passively absorb cultural products and the images of popular culture which the market forces and a multi-billion-dollar advertising industry dictate. More evidently, their perceptions and attitudes disclose a rejection of the use of cosmetics and a preference for traditional home made products.

With regard to the choice of products, these women decide and define for themselves how they would like to appear. In this process, although readymade things are available, they are not simply manipulated by the images infiltrating through the mass media. Preference for home-made products indicates clearly that they are really concerned about the safety and comfort of their body, be it hair or face or any other parts. This reveals their positive image[73] of beauty and body as an asset and power. Going by what convinces one certainly marks a point of agency and liberation. Moreover, when the unconventional women from the field refuse to fall a prey to the beauty myth, they reject men's institutionalized power in the spheres of female body and beauty.

By redefining beauty, the unconventional women challenge the existing conceptualizations of gender and the self. This redefinition challenges the strong moral stance that characterized earlier feminist works on beauty and physical appearance and the media-image of beauty; questions the unilateral characterization of beauty practices and physical appearance as oppressive; and challenges the conventional ideology of the female body as well as its standardized beauty, an ideal model 'Barbie Doll.'

In the context of a quest for self-affirmation, the accounts of these women who think differently about their care of beauty and appearance suggest that there is another side to women's appearance-practices: women *as active, assertive, and creative subjects* for their own satisfaction and enjoyment.

72. Cf. Kuhn, *The Power Of the Image*, 13.

73. Considering oneself or one's body as an asset leads to a positive image about oneself.

SEXUALITY AS AGENCY

Having explored the meaning of *agency* in the perceptions of unconventional women concerning their beauty care and physical appearance, the present section endeavors to investigate how these women exercise considerable autonomy to redefine their sexuality. The statistical analysis of the responses of the unconventional women brings to the fore how they resist the existing perception of male-defined marriage, kaṟpu, pati viratāi and female sexuality in a given patriarchal context. It is appropriate at this stage to understand the male-defined female sexuality in Tamil culture, in order to hermeneutically address the field data regarding body and sexuality.

Female Sexuality as a Site of Male Hegemony

Sexuality is part of every human being. From birth until death, every living being is a sexual being. "Unlike sex, sexuality is not confined to the bed; it is part of everyday life, it's your attitude," says Shiv Visvanathan, Sociologist at the Centre for the Study of Developing Societies in Delhi, India.[74] Thus sexuality involves the whole person.

However, in the Tamil context, female sexuality is tied to marriage. It is not only because it transforms a woman's status to adulthood (wife), but also because it brings her sexuality under the direct control of her husband to maintain the superior status of man.[75] Since in Dindigul district 'arranged marriages'[76] remain the rule, the possibilities for women to exercise autonomy with regard to their sexuality remain, by and large, unthinkable and difficult.[77]

However the analysis of the data reveals the elements of empowerment and autonomy which the unconventional women of the present study employ to take control of their body and sexuality. In a given context, how these women exercise their *agency* with regard to sexuality is our immediate concern.

74. As cited by Kala, "Beyond the Bed," 40.
75. Widge, Patriarchy, Social Control," 42.
76. 80 percent of our interviewees' marriages are arranged marriages.
77. Thapan, *Embodiment: Essays on Gender and Identity*, 181.

Refusal to be Male Chattels

In Tamil culture, a woman's (wife) body has been regarded as the field and man (husband) as the owner.[78] The husband becomes the owner of 'that' field through marriage. He ploughs this field and sows his seed in order to bring forth his progeny and to make the field productive. Almost all religions and cultures bolster the view of man's complete ownership of woman's body through marriage. For Manu, the woman's body is a field and man is the one who owns the field."[79] The biblical book of the first letter of St. Paul to the Corinthians 11:9 reads, "For the man is not of the woman; but the woman of the man. Neither was the man created for the woman; but the woman for the man."

In addition, the notion that a woman is the property of a man is also strongly imbedded in the soil of Tamils. What Anjali Widge has written about the condition of woman's body within marriage epitomizes the situation of women of Tamilnadu.

She writes:

> Perceived mostly as no more than a reproductive chamber, the female body has long been inscribed with elaborate codes of honor. Considered male property, to be protected or mauled, locked into passionless, abusive relationships, victimized by patriarchal sexual practices, whether during feudal exploitation, during caste atrocities, in communal riots, in policies regarding reproduction or in marital rape.[80]

These regressive realities are rampant still, but then it's equally valid that a growing number of women are challenging the dominantly male sexual order handed down to them. For example, one of the activists of AIDWA (All India Democratic Women's Association) openly said, "I am not his personal property to use when he wants and how he wants. I have my dignity." "This body is mine, not even my husband's," these oft-re-

78. Images of ownership are, of course, universal and originated in patriarchal feudalism. Levi-Strauss has commented on the matrimonial vocabulary of Great Russia, where the groom was called the 'merchant' and the bride the 'merchandise.' Cf. Strauss, *The Elementary Structures of Kinship*, 36; Cf. also Foucault, *The History of Sexuality*; Laqueur, *Making Sex*.

79. As cited in Kane, *History of Dharmasastras*, 200–1.

80. Widge, "Patriarchy, Social Control and the Female Body," 42; Cf. also the following authors who bring to light the situation of Indian women whose sexuality is being controlled by men. Kakar, *Intimate Relations*; Kapur, Love, *Marriage, Sex*; Misra and Radhika, eds., *Sexuality, Gender and Rights*.

peated phrases of the unconventional women of the present study imply that women are beginning to own their bodies; consequently, men are denied ownership over women's bodies. Such an attitude deconstructs the religious teachings and sacred texts, which maintain that women are created for men.[81]

When thrown into situations of sexual abuse, daring to say 'no' to oppressive relationships and deciding to live alone demonstrates women's agency leading to assertion. For the heterosexual women this may mean the loss of badly needed intimacy and marriage.[82] Still they are able to decide for themselves.

Defying Definitions

Another aspect of reclaiming their sexuality was manifested in women's courage to break the age-old myth of pati viratāi which is treated as sacred in the traditional understanding of Tamil marriage and family.

The land of Tamils has always upheld women who are pati viratāis. They have been honored and portrayed as models to be followed. The definitions of pati viratāi are found in several texts. While they differ marginally in their details, they all emphasize her existence as being husband-bound. For example, according to the Padma-purana "a pati viratāi is like a slave when at work, a courtesan when making love, like a mother when serving food, and a counselor when the husband is in distress." Likewise, the famous Tamil saying Kallāṉālum kaṇavaṉ pullāṉālum puruṣaṉ (he may be a stone or a blade of grass, he is your husband) insists on the wife's loyalty.

Chastity and wifely fidelity are the two important elements of the idealism put before women to aspire for. Manu describes a chaste wife as one who is pure and controlled in her mind, speech and body. She does not transgress her lord and thereby attaining her husband's region in the next life, for which she is exhorted to become like him already in this world by acquiring traits of mind and character similar to him.[83]

81. Cf. As cited in Montagu, *The Natural Superiority of Women*, 207.

82. In her book, Sheila speaks about the consequence of sexual revolution. For more details see Jeffreys, *Anticlimax: A Feminist Perspective*; Diamond and L. Quinby, eds., *Feminism and Foucault*.

83. Doniger, *The Laws of Manu –Maìusmrti*, Ch.9, Nos.12, 21 & 29.

But the perspective of unconventional women has begun to defy Manu's exhortation on a virtuous wife and wifely fidelity. What Karthigai[84] said regarding her opinion about wifely loyalty is highly significant to our context. "I do not want to waste my whole life with a drunkard. It's an artificial life. He drinks and beats me. After sometime he eats his food and I have to give in to his sexual desires because he has tied this tāli[85] and I am his wife. This is a stupid life. One day I threw him out."

'I don't need only a bed, I need a friend, a lover, who would be my co-traveler to the end,' seem to be the deeply felt and strongly articulated need of women. Thus a noteworthy change in the attitude of women is their newly acquired ability to break the long silence and to question the age-old practices with regard to female sexuality. Niranjana calls this form of resistance in the lives of women, 'an exercise of power.'[86] This confronts the wifely loyalty which Tamil culture has imposed mostly on women and the concept that the husband is a god to his wife and has complete power over her.

As women access more and more space in the private and the public sphere,—at offices, mills, factories, night-shifts, on roads, etc.—they take their sexuality with them everywhere and learn to be comfortable with it. It is apparent in Dindigul area that a growing number of women are beginning to challenge the dominantly male sexual order handed down to them. By refusing to be a traditional pati viratāi, these women take control of their lives and bodies and redefine sexuality.

Demolishing the Myth of kuṭumpa kauravam

Tamil feminist theoretician Rajam Krishnan has analyzed how in a Tamil patriarchal society, female sexuality is a site by which the morality of the family is determined, although it is not the case with men.[87] When a woman is raped, it is considered shameful and embarrassing not only to the victim but also to her family, especially for the male on whom she depends—her husband, father or brother. It is precisely for the same reason that women are raped during caste and communal

84. In personal communication with her at Dindigul—22.02.03. She is 38 and a professor in the college.

85. Tāli is a kind of chain or thread which the husband ties around his bride's neck on the day of the wedding.

86. Niranjana, *Gender and Space*, 88.

87. Cf. Krishnan, Kālam Tōrum Peṇmai (Women through the Years).

clashes.[88] Therefore to shame and to dishonor a family or a community, it is enough to abuse their women's bodies.

Thus a family's honor seems to be a female-linked commodity. Its preservation is incumbent upon the women's behavior alone. In the name of kuṭumpa kauravam, the female body has been colonized by patriarchal society. The obsession of Tamils with female sexual purity is a reflection of their anxieties about family honor and status and group boundaries (viz., family, caste, religious community, etc.). The institution of family plays an important role in colonizing the woman's body and sexuality, perpetuating its oppressive condition.

Hastrup aptly argued that the sexual state of women acts as a symbol of social purity: "It is a case of a biological model being used to serve distinct social purposes and for natural reasons it is the model of women's virginity that is of most use to society."[89]

In such a situation, when women decide to live single, they dare to go against the normal structure of family and society, and it breaks the institution of the family. Exercising the choice either to live with or to leave their husbands when they are physically abused, affects the kuṭumpa kauravam and social purity. Women remaining single or unmarried or separated from their husbands are sources of great tension to Tamils because the sexuality of these women does not come directly under the control of men. Moreover, women's preference for a single life[90] and their decision to move away from the constrained space and situation is an assertion of their right to self-actualization.

Deepa,[91] a rural dweller raised a pertinent question: "Is the woman only a body?" Deepa is now running a small hotel called 'Vasantha Bhavan,' after she walked out of her husband's house. She had to suffer maltreatment and humiliation from her husband and in-laws. "In the beginning I was looked down morally, and people even looked at me suspiciously. I was being ridiculed and cursed. Finding me alone, one man waved his fifty-rupee note to make his desire clear. My parents and especially my brother were very angry, blaming me saying that I am bringing damage to our family's reputation. I was flabbergasted. But I

88. See Sarkar, *Hindu Wife, Hindu Nation.*

89. Hastrup, "The Semantics of Biology," 56.

90. Among the respondents of the present study, 34 percent prefer to live a single than a married life.

91. In personal conversation with her at Thavasimedai—15.08.2005.

did not give up my goal. I cannot become anything for the sake of my family," she says with pride and self-dignity. A middle-aged woman now, she carries herself with dignity and is running a flourishing business.

What Deepti Kapoor states aptly fits in here:

> Unlike earlier days when women desired to marry for social status, security and procreation, today's women seek real companionship and intimacy. When they don't receive it they don't hesitate to move out. Moreover earlier they were hardly left with a choice due to economic dependence; today it's no more like that. Today, the economics of urban lifestyles has meant that many women are in situations where they do not need a prince charming to cart them off their feet.[92]

It is fitting also to quote here what a well-known Indian feminist writer Shobhaa De has said emphatically in one of her interviews:

> Today's women are in a position to say, 'Buddy, this is not what I want." Earlier, they could not. Because of their new financial empowerment, they can actually tell a man exactly where to get off. They are doing so with alarming alacrity, because they really do not need a man as a meal ticket any more. The big difference is that a man's role within marriage has not changed significantly. So it is the woman who repositioned herself at the workplace and at home on her terms.[93]

The unconventional women who reclaim their body and sexuality could well be defined in terms of Blanche Gelfant. By refusing to toe the line, to stay where they belong and by leaving home and men, they destabilize the family.[94] This leads to the redefinition of women's identity which is not always attached to the institution of a family. It is assumed that family is the place where women are supposed to be for their safety, morality and status.[95] When women move out of the family to live a life of their own, the institution of family collapses, and the established norms of sexual relationship is challenged. The notion that women cannot live without a family is disproved.

92. Kapoor, "Single & Swinging," 42.

93. Ibid.

94. Gelfant, "Sister to Faust," 23–38.

95. Bartky, *Femininity and Domination*; Millet, *Sexual Politics*.

Affirmation of Sexuality

Reclaiming sexuality is also clearly seen in women's attitude towards their need for sex, their courage to discuss sexual matters openly, their attitude towards marital symbols, etc. Sex in marriage is something a good woman is supposed to endure as part of her strī-tarmā.[96] "Tutored to be passive and submissive recipients of sex that men must initiate, women's sexual experiences, let alone their sexual aspirations, have rarely been issues at stake in our country," aptly observes Vrinda Nabar.[97] Although the weight of this attitude and practice is still pervasive in society, the unconventional women have begun to take initiative and articulate their need for sex. "I too have a body," "I too have needs," Such affirmations imply that the days of women's repressed sexuality seem to be fast disappearing, as women are prepared to take the initiative in matters of sex. Discussing issues concerning sex with their friends and husbands is a clear indication of women reclaiming the body and sexuality[98] in a society where the whole issue of sex is considered a taboo and a topic to be shunned.

Treating sexual feelings as normal as any other, is also highly important to women whose sexuality has been enslaved for centuries because this frees them from a sense of shame and makes them comfortable with themselves. Women coming out of their silence to assert their individuality and to recognize their sexual drive are beyond the comprehension of many in the society. Moving 'beyond the region of blind contentment,'[99] these women defy the conventional sanctions. This revalorizes the female body, rescuing it from the vilification which, for centuries, has been practiced against it through oppressive codes and institutions.

Besides, this disproves one of the important twentieth-century works on human and animal ethology which has followed the model of the active male and the passive female.[100] For example, Geddes and Thomson's observation on sex and sexuality in the famous book entitled *The Evolution of Sex* is as follows: "It is generally true that the males

96. Nabar, *Caste as Woman*, 38.

97. Ibid., 42.

98. Misra and Radhika, eds., *Sexuality, Gender and Rights*, 56.

99. Chopin, *The Awakening*, 742; Cf. also Marks and Isabelle, ed., *New French Feminisms*, 68–75.

100. This model is also embedded in Geddes and J. Arthur, *The Evolution of Sex*. The impact of this model is still prevalent in the Tamil society.

are more active, energetic, eager, passionate, and variable; the females more passive, conservative, sluggish, and stable."[101] Moreover, amidst the degradation of female sexuality, seeing one's own body as a source of potential power is necessary for the reclamation of female body.

Desertion of Marital Symbols

Female sexuality in Tamil culture is also tied around the marital symbols which women use. For instance, by custom, tāli is never removed from the body of the wife from the day of marriage till the death of her husband. A woman is supposed to wear the tāli always—day and night. It is usually removed from her neck on the death of her husband. And if her husband is alive when she dies then they bury her body along with the tāli to signify that having died as a tīrkka cumaṅkali,[102] she would attain mōkṣā immediately.

It is so striking that there are women who also redefine their sexuality by removing their tāli even when they are at home, while going for work, etc. It could, of course be argued that women might have removed the tāli because of some health problems. But what the author observed was a deliberate act—women doing it willfully and consciously. By deciding to remove the tāli, or by not wearing it regularly, or by not considering it as the foremost symbol in their lives, women decode the sacredness given to the tāli by culture.

Women deciding to resist the customary practices are an indication of the possibilities for agency in the midst of an experientially oppressive situation. Furthermore, such assertions also challenge the male prerogatives which are very often taken for granted. This also brings to light how patriarchal society uses tāli as a sacred tool to perpetuate male ownership of the woman's body. By questioning the age-old sacred symbol,[103] women overthrow the system that grants absolute power and control to men over their body as well as reclaim the ownership of their body.

Another important element that emerges here is that women no longer experience the cultural symbols as tools of safety and identity. Rather they see themselves beyond these symbols and derive their identity outside these symbols. This points to the fact that the value of cul-

101. Geddes and J. Arthur, *The Evolution of Sex*, 270.

102. A woman who dies before her husband is called as Tīrkka cumaṅkali.

103. Tāli has been considered as a sacred symbol of married women among Tamils.

tural symbols is beginning to lose its significance in the lives of both men and women. This changing perception of women questions the patriarchal construction of the female body—a body which is considered as weak and so it can be attacked by a demon / an evil spirit or any man. Women realize that their bodies are not physically weak and it is only a wrong assumption that was imposed on them. In addition, this calls into question the identity of women which is tied to the symbols of a male dominated world.

Redefining Femininity and Reclaiming Bodily Agency

It has already been brought to the fore how the perceptions of unconventional women concerning their bodies manifest elements of autonomy and freedom. However, it is in place to acknowledge here the importance of the identity formation of women. A number of books have testified in recent years as to how colonization of the body affects self-identity.[104] Identity is the stable, consistent, and reliable sense of who one is, and what one stands for in the world. It integrates one's meaning to oneself and to others.[105]

Christine E. Gudorf says, "Since our sense of self is grounded in our relationship to others, the experience of the body, both positive and negative, influences our self-identity.[106] If abuse and control of the body has an adverse impact on self, the positive affirmation of their bodies helps women to define their identities.

According to Ruthellen Josseleson, the most important developmental task facing women today is the formation of identity. For it is in the realm of identity that a woman bases her sense of herself as well as her vision of the structure of her life. Identity incorporates a woman's choices for herself, her priorities, and the guiding principles by which she makes decisions.[107] For the women of Dindigul district, who experience the colonization of their bodies through various ways in the given patriarchal context, redefining their identities through affirmation of their bodies (in the above mentioned ways) are clearly an indication of agency and empowerment.

104. See Russel, *The Secret Trauma*, 172–73.

105. See Josseleson, *Finding Herself*, 10.

106. Gudorf, "Body, Self and Sexual Identity," 9.

107. Josseleson, *Finding Herself*, 3.

To conclude, this chapter has attempted to interpret the meaning of *agency* found in the perceptions and attitudes of unconventional women of Dindigul district concerning their bodies. The analysis on the data has unearthed the unconventional women's desire to reclaim their body. Even as they face difficulties and disadvantages in their daily life situations, women negotiate and reclaim their bodies to shape their identities beyond the established understanding of motherhood, marriage, sexuality and beauty. When women have control over their body, they begin to live life to the full—their womanhood—humanhood—the ultimate aim of human life.

5

Female Agency: Negotiating Embodiment

THIS SECTION PRESENTS THE main findings of the book. In the light of the findings, some suggestions are also made for the formulation of a feminist theology of the body.

WOMEN AS DOUBLE SUBJECTS

A phenomenological and hermeneutic exploration into the perceptions of the women of Dindigul district, Tamilnadu, concerning their body clearly manifests both elements of *victimization* as well as elements of *agency*. In this sense, women are in a way, *double subjects*. The findings clearly indicate that a good number of them seem to accept the prevailing definitions of femininity and the female body, which they translate into their lives with an assumption of being *ideal women*.

However, the analysis of the data has also proved the hypothesis made by me at the beginning of this research. It is evident that there is a small section of women of Dindigul district who have begun to go against the existing conditionings of culture, religion and society. Privately and publicly, they exercise *autonomy* to reclaim their bodies despite the patriarchal norms that remain deeply embedded in Tamil culture. These women who exercise *agency* are referred to by me *as unconventional women*. Since the change of perception found in unconventional women differed at different phases of lives due to the impact of different variables, I am not able to give the exact number of unconventional women. Nevertheless, the statistical data pertaining to different areas in which the unconventional women exercise agency (based on qualitative data) are presented in the summary of the findings.

The first part of this chapter sums up the main findings in relation to the objectives and the hypothesis of the research. They are categorized and presented under thematic titles. The second part attempts to propose from a feminist point of view some theological reflections and implications derived from the findings.

SIGNIFICANT FINDINGS

Deprived 'agency'

With the arrival of feminist thinking and the impact of feminist movements, women are given opportunities / possibilities to exercise agency. However, the data from 62 percent of women from the present study clearly indicate that economic dependence and lack of exposure continue to keep them submissive to the existing perceptions of socio-cultural and religious practices concerning their body, namely motherhood, dress code, space, sexuality, beauty, etc. Moreover, it is these women (who are economically dependent) who are the heralds of conventional perceptions.

Nexus between kuṭumpa kauravam *and the Female Body*

The findings disclose that kuṭumpa kauravam determines the space and freedom of the female body. The responses from 68 percent of the participants proved the nexus between the disciplining of woman's body and kuṭumpa kauravam. Since a sense of shame is linked to kuṭumpa kauravam, often it takes precedence over women's freedom and autonomy.

Fragmented notion of Body and Sexuality

The statistical analysis of the socio-cultural perceptions of women of Dindigul district concerning body and sexuality reveals that, on the whole, religion and its sacred scriptures play a greater role in the construction of existing female sexuality. Moreover, the findings also disclose that the Christian women are quite narrow in their attitude towards their body and sexuality when compared to women of other religions. The Christian women, in spite of their higher education and occupation, continue to uphold the traditional religious teachings on body and sexuality. The responses of 82 percent of Christian women concerning body and sexuality confirm this.

The Intertwining of the Political Economy and Perceptions of Body

One of the significant findings of this book is that when the concern is survival, women do not hesitate to undo the social conditionings on their body. In the face of severe economic deprivation, the women of the present study struggle for survival and subsistence. As a result, they dare to break the patriarchal norms that demarcate their body space. This was seen in 58 percent of the respondents. The concern for survival is much more a daunting issue for women who are thrown into such a situation than living up to the expectations of society.

Refusal to Male Hegemony

Down the centuries, in the Tamil context, marriage has been made almost inevitable for most women. And the notion of a woman's chastity is particularly considered as sacrosanct in the context of Tamil marriages. In this milieu, the whole understanding of marriage on the part of women as one of tolerance in case of abuse and disloyalty is taking a different turn among these women. Among 42 percent of the women, a preference to live alone when met with disloyalty on the part of their husbands seems to take precedence over the preservation of cultural practices and kuṭumpa kauravam.

Redefining Beauty

The experience of beauty as an element of agency and power is seen among 49 percent of the unconventional women. The reason for their beauty care and appearance does not confine itself to please the *gaze of others*; but it gives birth to an alternative discourse which considers beautifying one's body as an elaborated expression of who one is and what one can become. The accounts of these women suggest how beauty care can enable women to be active, assertive, competent and creative subjects of their own satisfaction and enjoyment.

Deconstructing Motherhood

In a context where motherhood is considered as a highest position for some, 46 percent of the respondents have begun to look at their bodies beyond motherhood. This points to the fact that women not only begin to redefine their body beyond motherhood but also deconstruct the stereotypes of patriarchy that limits the role of a woman's body to mere childbearing. The emerging consciousness of these women to contribute to the world in a significantly broader capacity than that of being a mother can be a pointer for other women too, especially for women who are issueless.

Spatiality as Agency

The data from 71 percent of the respondents who work outside confirms that the expansion of physical space plays a significant role among the women of Dindigul district. Moving out from the known to the unknown space, either for work or for education or for survival increases their knowledge about their body in particular and life in general. They are able to break the conventional classifications and violate the prescribed norms to find a new space with a new identity of their own. However, the findings also disclose that access to physical spaces alone does not bring about empowerment, but rather it depends on the *quality* of that space.

Power of the Collectives

The many substantive changes in the attitude towards their bodies found among the women of the present study can be attributed to the impact of action-oriented groups that have focused on cultural deconstruction. 51 percent of those involved in action-oriented groups claim that different awareness programs conducted in these groups have given them a *new type of consciousness* to come out of their insulated enclosures and social spaces, expressing their equality, freedom and dignity in relation to men. Besides, the elements of this transformation among women include empowerment, self-confidence, socio-cultural and political consciousness and assertion of self-identity leading to agency. This suggests that economic empowerment alone does not bring about a change of perception of oneself. Rather, women need enlightenment in this process which can be accelerated through cultural deconstruction and reconstruction.

Education as a Catalyst of Empowerment

Another factor which has served as a catalyst towards the empowerment of unconventional women is higher education. 59 percent of those who have been highly educated and employed disclose that higher education has opened their minds, effecting considerable change on the perception of their bodies. It has enhanced their self-esteem and self-confidence building a sense of positive self-worth. Nevertheless, these changes are mostly dependant on *the place, quality, type and duration* of education and what the women do with it later.

Employment Coupled with Economic Freedom

Gainful work has helped women to enjoy economic independence, to get exposed to the world outside, to gain knowledge of their bodily abilities, to be self-assertive, and to grow in self-affirmation. The data from 57 percent of those employed and enjoying economic freedom disclose a progressive attitude and a greater consciousness of themselves. It has enabled them to grow in personal freedom and psychological power. It has given them more confidence, status, popularity and prestige. Thus, employment alone is not sufficient for women's empowerment; they must be able to own the money that they earn.

Dalits: Agents "making" a difference

Traditional Tamil society governed by the caste system and the patriarchal joint family system accord the lowest position to the scheduled castes and a far inferior position to their women in society.[1] The status of dalit women is inferior and impure in society as well as in their families.[2] But, the responses of 55 percent of dalit women show that they seem to negate whatever society considers impure regarding the body. Rather they treat it as power, well-being, source of happiness and goodness. This *power from within* with which dalit women move around and exercise *agency* is indeed a positive move towards the liberation of dalit women and the transformation of society as well.

The Media: An Agent of Systemic Change

The role of the media often has been undermined and is often blamed for victimizing women through its ads and serials. Contrary to the gen-

1. At the time of birth, a scheduled caste woman is asked to look after the cleanliness of the place where a woman is kept in confinement. At the time of marriage, the scheduled caste women are called upon to perform certain menial services of carrying and disposing of the waste. At the time of some one's death, the message is conveyed to relations only by a messenger who is an untouchable, because the very idea of death is looked upon as impure. Cf. Jain et al., *Scheduled Caste Women*, 16–17.

2. Ibid.

eral notion that the media perpetuates the traditional gender roles and promotes and reinforces unrealistic ideals of male hegemony, we can see the affirmative role which the media has played from the responses of 34 percent of those who view them regularly. They have enabled them to have a right motivation for their beauty care and to take control of their body and sexuality by freeing them from inhibition and from a sense of shame.

To sum up, autonomy and the element of agency were seen both among women who are economically well-off and those in the lower strata of society. In the case of women who are economically well-off, it is education, employment and economic empowerment and exposure to the media that have enabled them to exercise autonomy. In the case of women who are economically poor, it is the situation of economic survival and the impact of action-oriented groups that make them exercise autonomy. Above all, exposure to a new space has empowered women of all categories to a certain extent.

Thus, the findings from the field study among the women of Dindigul district disclose both women who appear passive, lacking agency, waiting for a definition from *others* and a small active and empowered section, involved in deconstruction and reconstruction of cultural conditionings on their body. The possibilities of *women's agency* in negotiating their identity through their bodies are endless. If women are consciously aware of their active and lived relationship to their bodies, they can exercise agency which is central to their embodied existence.

SALIENT CONTRIBUTIONS

The book offers three specific contributions regarding methodology to feminism and feminist theology in India and Asia at large.

A Contextual Study in Feminism

Studies on women have been, to a large extent, done around certain theoretical and ideological frameworks. While recognizing the important contribution of western feminism, it should be noted that in India, the condition of women is not simply an outcome of an ideology. In the Indian context, it is highly important to analyze and examine how women are subjugated and exploited through the power of traditions and socio-cultural and religious practices.

The present study has tried precisely to locate the treatment of women's body in a distinct socio-cultural situation prevailing in the district of Dindigul, Tamilnadu, India. The book has gone into the perceptions of women's body not from any ideological framework, but from their socio-cultural and economical context. The book has phenomenologically presented the self-perceptions of women regarding their body at different phases of their lives. Further, it has explored the various factors that influence their perceptions and has made an attempt to view them hermeneutically, bringing to the fore the elements of *agency* that women exercise to reclaim their bodies.

Women's Bodies in Gender Studies

Although studies on women have entered the academia, books concerning women's bodies are very few. The present study, though it comes under the broad umbrella of feminist studies, makes a definite contribution to feminism by having women themselves speak about their perception of their bodies.

Women As Agents

By and large in Western and Indian feminist writings, attention has been focused on the oppression and marginalization of women. On the whole, there is a general silence on how women become agents to take control of their own bodies in patriarchal society. This book did not confine itself to examine the factors and forces that keep them under subjugation. It went a step further to see whether and to what extent women themselves play roles and use strategies to go against the conventional practices and customs regarding their body. This book has attempted to identify the elements of *agency* which women exercise to reclaim their bodies, namely the strategies that women use to defy the cultural hegemony and to redefine their identities *beyond the expected and set roles.*

Keeping in view these findings I arrive at some conclusions and recommendations to initiate the process of empowerment of women through an appropriate feminist theology.

CONTEXTUAL FEMINIST THEOLOGY

Feminist theology is contextual and is based on the experiences of women 'here and now.'[3] Feminist theology emerged with the recognition that traditional theology is grounded in the experience of men. The concerns of the world of women become the core of feminist theological studies. As such, theology is in no way disassociated from the discipline of sociology.[4] In this section, the author identifies some of the issues that emerged from this socio-cultural study and provides some pointers for the reformulation of theology in general and feminist theology in particular.

Before we move on to propose suggestions for feminist theology, let us have a look at the state of the female body in Christian theology.

Female Body in Christian Theology: An Overview

If we examine the Christian tradition of the theology of body, what we learn is something very complex, ambiguous and paradoxical. Certainly, Christianity under the influence of a philosophical dualism negated the body as something low, while exalting the soul as high.

There are many expressions of this trend. For example, body, sexuality and emotions are all seen as potentially uncontrollable forces and as sources of great anxiety.[5] As a result, there has been penal punishment of the body, ascetic practices and disciplining of the body and violations against one's own body. This was thought to be imperative to kindle the spirit and keep alive the union of the soul with God. As Peter Brown has shown in his masterly work on sexual renunciation in early Christianity,[6] Christians came to focus much more insistently on the body and the repression of its needs for food, sleep and sexual urges than pagan ascetics.

Moreover, the culture of patriarchy into which both Judaism and Christianity were born affirmed the normativity and superiority of men. Women and their bodies were regarded as dangerous sources of unclean-

3. According to Catherina Halkes, feminist theology is committed to factual analysis and an inspiration based on faith. Cf. Halkes, "Feminist Theology," 114.

4. Wilfred, *On the Banks of Ganges*, 7; Idem, *The Sling of Utopia*, 13–14; Cf. also Rahner, *Theological Investigations—Vol.9*, 28.

5. Brown, *The Body and Society*.

6. Cf. Ibid.

ness. When this mentality met with Greek dualism which associated the rational with the male and the non-material and women with nature, the stage was set for the emergence of a body-denying theology.[7]

The approach to the woman's body needs to be seen in the context of this overall orientation. There is even an identification of the body itself with women—the body of the woman was seen in competition with God in winning the souls of men. With this was connected the whole interpretation of the story of Genesis wherein the woman becomes the tempting Eve—deflecting man from his spiritual pursuit.

Women were equated with insatiable sexuality and irrationally demonic temptation. There was a systematic denigration of women in order to attract men to a life of celibacy. Sexual union was projected into a mystical realm of erotic spirituality, and endless commentaries on the Song of Songs—the favorite biblical text of the medieval period—invited men to direct their longings to the one safe woman, Mary, the perpetual virgin.[8]

Celibacy became the ideal and marriage became the refuge for those who could not cope with celibacy. Virgins, widows and wives were seen as three rungs on a ladder of virtue.

The following text underscores the hatred with which the monks wrote when they refused to work with women.

> We and our whole community of canons, recognizing that the wickedness of women is greater than all the other wickedness of the world, and that there is no danger like that of women, and that the poison of asps and dragons is more curable and less dangerous to men than the familiarity of women, have unanimously decreed for the safety of our souls, no less than for that of our bodies and goods, that we will on no account receive any more sisters to the increase of our perdition, but will avoid them like poisonous animals.[9]

Women were kept out of the public gaze, because the very sight of a woman's body would arouse men's lust, cause discord, violence, adul-

7. Thatcher and Elisabeth ed., *Christian Perspectives on Sexuality*, ix–x.

8. Malone, *Women & Christianity*, 54.

9. Abbot Conrad of Marchtal, quoted in Southern, *Western Society and the Church*, 22.

tery and revenge. Even when obeying church law, women attending the Sunday service were seen as 'arsonists of sacred places.'[10]

At the beginning of the modern age, women were considered as evil and were called devils or witches in order to signify the evil that they supposedly embodied. The ensuing period of witch-hunting, when the Churches identified the *witches* and burnt their bodies at the stake, is one of the most atrocious periods of Christian history. These were the negative consequences of a dual Christian anthropology which identified man with the mind and woman with the body.

These negative attitudes towards the body on the whole and the woman's body in particular were not the only elements found in Christian tradition. There has been as well a strong Christian tradition that affirmed an anthropology which was wholistic. Human persons were seen as an organic reality in which body and mind flow into each other and are constantly in interaction with each other. The theology of the incarnation, far from seeing the body as something contrary to the goal of salvation views in it the very hinge of salvation—*caro cardo salutis*.

There was a deeper understanding of the mystery of the human body as the symbol of divine presence. Not surprisingly then, the transfiguration of the body and its resurrection were viewed as integral parts of salvation. The sacramentality of the human body and its place in Christian tradition is exemplified in the firm belief in the resurrection. Moreover, it was the conviction about the salvific role of the body that made Christian believers have a great veneration to the relics of martyrs and saints. They became objects of great devotion, cult and pilgrimage. The analysis has highlighted the presence of two approaches to the body in Christian tradition, negative and positive.

The study of feminist theologians[11] has clearly shown that the negative outlook on the body has found precedence in the understanding of women's body. As we have noted already, this has had multiple repercussions on the very status of women. Unfortunately, the other traditions based on the incarnation, the resurrection and the veneration of relics

10. A good number of writers held the same view at this time. They include Alan of Lille, James of Vitry, Vincent of Beauvais, William Peraldo, Gilbert of Tournai and John of Wales. For more details cf. also Casagrande "The Protected Woman," 85.

11. Cf. Reuther, "Re-evaluating the Body," 41–49; Quinn, "Body Culture,"; Teresa Berger, "Woman as Alien Bodies,"; Menne, "Catholic Sexual Ethics,"14–25; Bynum, *Fragmentation and Redemption*.

of saints and martyrs had not made any positive impact on Christians' attitude towards the body in general and woman's body in particular.

Western feminist movements and feminist theology have made legitimate protests against the dominant traditions of dualism, of the negation of the body and the misinterpretation of the Genesis story. All the same, substantial efforts have not been undertaken by Christianity to liberate women in general and their bodies in particular from the contemporary social situation.

TOWARDS A REFORMULATION OF FEMINIST THEOLOGY

The three crucial issues that have emerged from the book are the following: *Reclaiming the body, redefinition of sexuality and re-visioning space.* Theology in general and feminist theology in particular will benefit from incorporating these elements to formulate a theology that might lead to the right understanding of the body as well as the liberation of women who are still victimized.

Evolving a Body-Affirming Theology

The present book has highlighted the fact that not all women are passive and subservient to the situation of oppression. There are some who have begun to exercise *agency* in order to reclaim their bodies in a given oppressive situation. This could certainly be a point of reference for the formulation of a theology of the body.

Evolving a theology which affirms human bodies entails moments of celebration and intimate relationships leading to the rediscovery of the body as a God-given gift. It creates a positive attitude in woman to her body, filling her with a sense of wonder and reverence leading to reclamation and affirmation of the self. Moreover, a theology of the body deconstructs and reconstructs the myths that humiliate and destroy bodies both in Christianity and in other religions.

The positive approach to the body which we have already identified above could also contribute to the development of a theology of the body. This theology of the body could draw inspiration from theological and spiritual resources which underline the incarnation, the resurrection and the veneration of the relics of martyrs, in which there is no distinction between male and female. There is a commonality found in these traditions, going beyond sex and gender. St. Paul speaks of this in his letter, "There is no longer Jew or Greek, there is no longer slave or free, there is no longer male and female; for all of you are one in Christ Jesus" (Gal 3:28).[12] In Christ, the dividing orders of male/female, mind/body, higher/lower, pure/impure, superior/inferior are broken. Speaking about the commonality among all sexes after the resurrection Jesus said, "Those who belong to this age marry and are given in marriage; but those who are considered worthy of a place in that age and in the resurrection from the dead, neither marry nor are given in marriage" (Lk 20:34–35). Hence going beyond the divisions that separate the human bodies on the basis of sex should be one of the concerns of the theology of body.

Further, a theology of the body should also promote women's bodily agency rather than victimization. This involves honoring women's bodily power not only as procreators but also as embodied and powerful persons of the Divine as St. Paul would say, "Do you not know that you are God's temple and that God's Spirit dwells in you? If anyone destroys God's temple, God will destroy that person. For God's temple is holy, and you are that temple" (1 Cor 3:16–17).[13] The awareness of the indwelling of the Holy Spirit in a human body is in a way an invitation not only to feel good about one's own body but also to give due respect to that body. Therefore, anyone who violates this body violates the image of God.

Moreover, Christian theology ought to use its own particular methods to reformulate the question of women's liberation and feminism in relation to the doctrine of God. This requires the revision of a great deal of the Judaeo-Christian tradition, which has often been anti-feminist in its approach because of its androcentric, masculinist and even machistic view of the world. Hence, it is also essential to identify the elements of liberation hidden in the sacred scripture in order to help women to reclaim and affirm their body.

12. All the biblical passages used in this section are taken from *The New Revised Standard Version* (Nashville: Thomas Nelson Publishers, 1990).

13. Some of the other similar passages of St. Paul are "Do you not know that your body is a temple of the Holy Spirit within you, which you have from God and that you are not your own?" (1 Cor 6:19); "What agreement has the temple of God with idols? For we are the temple of the living God; as God said, "I will live in them and walk among them, and I will be their God, and they shall be my people." (2 Cor 6:16).

Evolving a Theology of Sexuality

The negative teachings of the Church on the body have led to the narrow outlook on women and sexuality as degrading. Women's bodies were viewed as objects of distraction and properties of men.

Feminist theologians have attempted to bring to light the Church's attitude towards female sexuality.

For example, Rosemary Ruether states:

> Women are seen both as creatures to be put on a pedestal as 'beyond' sexual feelings and as sexual objects to be used and discarded. If women themselves become agents of their own sexual activity, making their own decisions about both when and how to enjoy sex and how to limit its reproductive effects on their bodies, they are seen as disgraceful sinners who must be punished and forced to submit to male definitions of their sexual roles.[14]

In the same way, Asian woman theologian Kwok Pui-lan too writes, "As the descendants of Eve, women are seen as potential seductresses or temptresses, and their sexuality has to be brought under the control of the patriarchal family or church."[15] Due to this unhealthy outlook on sex, Rosemary Ruether writes, "Sex is disdained as beneath respectability and exploited pornographically, both of which privilege men over women."[16] The data from the Christian women of the present study have also disclosed the damaging understanding of sexuality as something evil and sinful. In the given situation, reconstructing a theology which presents a wholistic view of human sexuality is imperative.

Jesus conveys powerfully the meaning of sexuality among the married couple. He says, "Have you not read that the one who made them at the beginning 'made them male and female,' and said, 'For this reason a man shall leave his father and mother and be joined to his wife, and the two shall become one flesh'? So they are no longer two but one flesh" (Matt 19:4–6). Thus Jesus created a "new language" to break the silence and reversed the demeaning approach towards body and sexuality.

A theology of sexuality should take into consideration the affirmation of one's own sexuality. It should also encompass one's total self-expression to others in relationship. It encourages the celebration of

14. Ruether, "Sex in the Catholic Tradition," 35–36.

15. Pui-lan, *Introducing Asian Feminist Theology*, 118.

16. Ibid., 51.

body and sexuality which brings together the three aspects of Christian love: *eros, phile* and *agape*.

This theology of sexuality should also revise the criteria by which an act of sex is to be judged as moral or immoral. An act of sex is immoral to the degree it is violent, abusive and lacks commitment. Likewise, sex could be moral to the degree that the couple grows into greater love and friendship, commitment and mutuality.[17] Such a view would revolutionize the traditional attitudes within married heterosexual relationship which allows men to exploit and violate women's bodies. Hence what is needed for the Church is to promote a new *ars erotica* in order to help people develop their capacity for sexual pleasure and enjoyment while integrating it into a deepening friendship, so that sex becomes increasingly an expression of love, commitment and caring that seeks to be mutual.

Asian feminist theologians affirm women's sexuality as integral and important parts of their spirituality.[18] Therefore the approach to spirituality should be not one of self-denial, focused on the suppression of one's own desire, but of acknowledging, appreciating and affirming one's own body and self.

Evolving a Theology of Spatiality

Space is that which allows a person the place/freedom/margin to do what she/he intends to do. Space is that which allows a person to move, maneuver and negotiate one's identity. There are physical, mental, economic, socio-cultural and political spaces. The stimuli for empowerment come when something alters in a woman's life which expands spaces.

As already stated among the findings as well as by the criteria set by Joy Deshmukh, who treats spaces as indicators of power and empowerment, extension of *physical space* has been a tool of power and empowerment of unconventional women to assert their bodies, especially in the given context. Through *higher education, employment, active participation in movements, exposure to urban centers*, etc., these women have been able to expand their physical space. In all these spheres, expansion of *mental space* has facilitated the generation of a 'power within'—which is an important requirement for the empowerment of women.

17. Rosemary Ruether, "Sex in the Catholic Tradition," 50.

18. Pui-lan, *Introducing Asian Feminist Theology*, 131.

Mental space[19] allows women to understand the injustices that they face and enables them *to operate through collectives*, such as the family, a specific laboring class, caste or economic status group, etc. Hence, being a part of collectives facilitates the process of empowerment among women. Another factor that has helped in the expansion of mental space is *knowledge*. It has been an important source of power as well as an instrument to exercise agency. Most often women's bodies are abused because they are illiterate and ignorant. Knowledge achieved through higher education and awareness programs is most critical to unleash a process of empowerment among women. Another kind of knowledge that is vital is *information about rights and duties* both as citizens of civic society and as members of family and Church. The present study has shown that self-confidence and self-esteem in women has increased with the expansion of *mental space*.

This clearly indicates that theologizing spatiality could also be a tool of women's empowerment. This implies creating space for women through education, employment, participation in public and Church activities, movements, etc. in order that they may grow as full human beings.

Women can draw inspiration from the life of Jesus who provided opportunities for the women of his time with an *expansion of mental space.* He affirmed women who transgressed the conventional space. In general, as in most of the cultures, the kitchen was considered the primary space for Jewish women. Women have very little access to the public space, and their physical mobility is curtailed by and large. When Mary of Bethany transgressed this space in order to pursue her personal interest, Jesus affirmed her positively by saying, "Mary has chosen the better part, which will not be taken away" (Lk 10:42b). In the same way, the well is not the place for men. Jesus meets the Samaritan woman in her space in order to lead her to a greater space (Jn 4:1ff). When Mary of Magdala trespassed the space of men to wash the feet of Jesus, he affirms her by approving her act publicly and rewards her with eternal life (Matt 26:6–13).

In order to effect a healthy change among women with regard to their body, the feminist movements today need to take up the task of *expanding the mental space of women.* Developing mental space—a space that facilitates the generation of a 'power within'- is more important than just giving women economic and political space.

19. I attempt to apply the effects of *mental space* as proposed by Joy Deshmukh–Ranadive, to the unconventional women of Dindigul district. Ranadive, *Space for Power.*

Conclusion

The key finding of the book is that the female body is not only the site of violence, exclusion, exhibition and abuse but also the site for agency which allows for the possibilities of negotiation, intervention, contestation and transformation. Women are continuously in the making in the process of communication and exchange, while going through their day-to-day life experiences. In the process of reclaiming *the sacredness of the body and power in sexuality* and *through a redefinition of beauty*, women take possession of their embodied selves, thus, negotiating their subjectivity in the given context. It is in this sense that the body becomes a vehicle for the human making and remaking of the world, always shifting sites, empowered with the potential for opening up new possibilities of being in this world.

This study comes as a boost to women who are oppressed while at the same time challenging thoroughly the patriarchal attitude of the oppressors of women. The unconventional women of Dindigul District, Tamilnadu, India become possible role models for women who are voiceless, helpless and victimized to grow in assertion and affirmation of their bodies and identities.

The book also affirms the contribution of action-oriented groups who play a significant role in empowering these rural women. Further, it demands the attention of the NGOs, SHGs, Policy makers, feminists and all those who are truly concerned about the empowerment of women and the establishment of equality at all levels of the Church and Society to encourage and facilitate the process of women exercising bodily empowerment and agency.

Appendix I

Survey Questionnaire

Women's Perception of their Body, Dindigul District

Please Note: Your answers will be used for study purpose only. It will not be revealed to anyone at any time or occasion.

Date:

Sl. No.:

Age:

- 21–30
- 31–40
- 40–45

Education:

- Illiterate
- 1st–5th Std.
- 6th–12th Std.
- Graduate

Occupation:

- Unorganized
- Organized
- Unemployed (Housewife)

Religion:

- Hindu
- Christian
- Islam

Caste:

- BC
- MBC
- SC

Domicile:

- Rural
- Urban

Family Status:

- Below 2000
- 2000-5000
- 5000 and above (monthly income)

Nature of the Family:

- Nuclear
- Joint

Frequency of Use of Media:

- Daily
- Once a Week
- Rarely
- Never

Member of an Action-Oriented Group:

- Yes
- No

A. BODY AND MENSTRUATION

What is your first experience of menstruation?	
Did you have the celebration when you attained puberty?	YES/NO
What was your feeling? Were you happy to celebrate or felt humiliated?	
What is your perception of puberty rite?	
Were you separated during your first menstruation?	YES/NO
How many days and where were you staying away?	
What did you feel during those days?	
Do you stay outside even now during menstruation? Why?	YES/NO
Your religion says that woman's body is impure (tīṭṭu) during menstruation. Do you consider your body impure during menstruation? Why?	YES/NO
What do you mostly feel during menstruation? Why?	
a)Proud and good	
b)Uneasy	
c)Ashamed Off	
d)Irritated	
e)Any other	
Do you talk about it with other women? To your husband?	YES/NO
Do you avoid going to temple? Why?	YES/NO
If you go to temple what will happen?	
What are the things that you avoid during menstruation? Why?	
Do you find it difficult to work during menstruation?	YES/NO
Do you take care of your body during menstruation?	YES/NO
What is your opinion about women who have not attained puberty?	

B. BODY AND MARRIAGE

Do you think that a woman's body finds its fulfilment only through marriage?	YES/NO
By tying tāli,, does your husband claim right over your body?	YES/NO
Is your husband the owner of your body?	YES/NO
Why do we use marital symbols like tāli, meṭṭi and kuṅkumam?	
Do you find these marital symbols meaningful? How?	YES/NO
Do you use them regularly? Why?	YES/NO
Do you find that marriage controlling your bodily movements?	YES/NO
Suppose you are asked to choose a life, what life would you prefer to live?	
a) Married Life	
b) Single Life	
c) Spinster	

C. BODY AND CHASTITY

According to you what is chastity?	
In Tamil society especially in films, a woman who is raped or molested marries mostly the culprit even if she has no liking towards him. What is your opinion of it?	
Is chastity associated with a body?	YES/NO
Should a woman preserve her body from being touched or abused by men before marriage? Can a wife relate to another man when the husband is unfaithful to her?	YES/NO
Suppose when you happen to hear that your husband is having an extra marital relationship, how will you respond?	
Should the society insist on men's chastity?	YES/NO
Is chastity needed only before marriage?	YES/NO

If chastity is nothing to do with body but only with self-control and being faithful to one's commitment to life, can a woman who is forced into prostitution, be considered as chaste?	YES/NO
Is Kannagi a perfect model for a Tamil woman?	YES/NO
What is your opinion about Madhavi?	
What do you think of the popular saying kallāṉālum kaṇ avaṉ pullāṉālum puruṣaṉ? Should women follow this saying strictly?	

D. BODY AND MODESTY

Is modesty meant only for women?	YES/NO
When do you call a woman, modest?	
Is it when she covers her body/face properly or ties hair properly when she goes outside?	YES/NO
Do you like to cover your body and face with purdah?	YES/NO
Do you use purdah to cover your face? a) Always b) Sometimes c) Never	
Is modesty lies in woman's way of walk, speech and laugh?	YES/NO
What is modesty for you?	
What is your opinion about the popular saying Accamu m, maṭamum, nāṇamum, payirppum niccamum peṇp ārkkuriyatu.	

E. BODY AND SEXUALITY

Do you feel proud to be a woman? Why?	YES/NO
Who is the owner of your body? Why?	
What is your attitude towards body and sexuality?	
How do you feel about your body parts?	
Do you like your body parts?	YES/NO
What is sexuality for you?	
Which way does your body make you a woman?	

Does your body have sufficient freedom to do what it wants?	YES/NO

F. BODY AND SEXUAL RELATIONSHIPS

What is sexual relationship for you?	
Are you aware of your bodily and sexual needs?	YES/NO
Do you take initiative to use your body to express love?	
a) Often	
b) Rarely	
c) Never	
Do you use your body to express love to your husband in a non-sexual way?	YES/NO
When you express your need for intimacy, how does your husband respond?	
a) accepts it	
b) rejects it	
c) any other	
Are you obliged to give pleasure for your husband always ?	YES/NO
Do you think that your body is created to give pleasure for a man?	YES/NO
What do you feel when you are unable to satisfy your husband sexually?	
1) Fear	
2) Sadness	
3) Indifference	
4) Guilt	
5) Normal	
6) Any Other	
Do you have the freedom to say 'no' when you are not in disposition?	YES/NO
Do you enjoy sexual intimacy?	YES/NO
What do you feel when your sexual needs are not given sufficient attention by your husband?	
Are you conscious of it?	YES/NO

Do you talk to your husband about your sexual needs?	YES/NO
Have you any time felt that you are wanted by your husband only for sex?	YES/NO
Do you give into his desires always?	YES/NO
Are you afraid that if you don't satisfy him, he might look for another?	YES/NO
Do you feel that your body is being abused by your husband, just because he has tied tāli for you?	YES/NO
Do you talk about your sexual feelings to your women friends?	YES/NO
Is having sex outside the marriage, sinful?	YES/NO
What is your opinion about extra marital affair when your marriage is not a satisfying one?	

G. BODY AND MOTHERHOOD

Do you have a say in planning your family especially with regard to number of children?	YES/NO
Do you consider motherhood as very essential for you?	YES/NO
Do you have the freedom not only to prevent or end unwanted pregnancy but also whether and when to have children?	YES/NO
Do you feel that you are pressurised to be responsible for birth control?	YES/NO
What did you feel when you came to know that you have become pregnant?	
a) happy and fulfilled	
b) anxious	
c) sad	
d) any other	
What was your feeling during pregnancy?	
a) Proud	
b) Uneasy and Embarrassed	
c) Burden	
d) Uninterested	
e) Any Other	
Is your body impure during child-birth?	YES/NO

What is your opinion about abortion?	
What do you feel about breast-feeding?	
Do you feel happy or shy to breastfeed?	
Does it affect your beauty?	YES/NO
Do you avoid breastfeeding your child for any purpose?	YES/NO
Does Woman's body find fulfilment only in Motherhood?	YES/NO
What is your experience of being a mother?	
a) Pleasant	
b) Burdensome	
c) Any other	
What do you feel when you see women who do not exercise their motherhood / a barren woman / Unwed mothers?	
a) Sad	
b) Normal	
c) Indifferent	
d) Any Other	
Is your womb precious to you?	YES/NO
Is it just like any other organ?	

H. BEAUTY AND PHYSICAL APPEARANCE

Is physical beauty more important than intelligence for a woman?	YES/NO
Does physically beautiful woman have better opportunities in life?	YES/NO
Are you conscious of your physical appearance? a) Always b) Sometimes c) Never	
Are you satisfied with your bodily structure?	YES/NO
Do you look for tips from magazines or go to beauty parlours to improve your physical appearance? Do you dress up well? Is so, why?	
a) To please my husband	
b) To feel good about myself	

c) To attract others	
d) To pursue a carrier	
e) Any other	
How do you take care of your body?	
Do you usually go in for home made tips / ready made cosmetics?	YES/NO
What are the home-made / ready-made products you use to beautify?	
Are you conscious of your colour? a) Always b) Sometimes c) Never	
Should women waste money and time on beauty at all?	
Is woman's beauty meant for a man?	YES/NO
Are you conscious of your weight?	YES/NO
Do you reduce/ forego meals to keep your body slim?	YES/NO
Are you forced to look beautiful?	YES/NO
Do you compare yourself with the other with regard to beauty?	YES/NO
Should a widow give up her bodily decorations? Why?	YES/NO
What is beauty for you?	
Have you been doubted anytime because you dressed up well?	YES/NO

I. BODILY MOBILITY AND SPACE

Is your body meant to be inside the house? Why?	YES/NO
Do you go out in the night without a male company?	YES/NO
Do you think that women who go out 'freely' are immoral in their behaviour?	YES/NO
Is your body weak? Can it be easily attacked by a man or by an evil spirit?	YES/NO
Is your body safe outside /when you travel / when you go for work?	YES/NO
Suppose when a male visitor comes to see your husband, will you also sit with him and talk? Or when he comes when your husband is out, where do you stand and talk to him?	

Do you go out freely without being accompanied by your husband other than for your work? Should women expand their space? Or is it enough that they mind the business within their homes? Do you go to a hotel or a tea shop and have a cup of coffee or tea alone? Why?	YES/NO
Do you find your body being abused inside the home / outside the home?	

J. BODY AND LABOUR

Are you physically over strained by work?	YES/NO
Can your body work longer?	YES/NO
Should women take up light works since they are biologically weak?	
Is your body an obstacle for you to do anything?	YES/NO
What can be done to make your body stronger?	
Do you think that men are biologically stronger than women?	YES/NO
Does physical appearance matters for a woman at her work-spot?	YES/NO
Is your body safe in your work place?	YES/NO
Have you anytime used your body and beauty to pursue a career / job?	YES/NO
Work is a	
a) burden	
b) pleasure	
c) self-growth	

Your contribution will be an eye-opener to our patriarchal society.
Thank you very much.

Appendix II

Profile of the Respondents of Quantitative Data

Table 1.1: Distribution of the respondents by their religion

Religion	Frequency	Percent
Hindu	189	37.8
Christian	186	37.2
Muslim	125	25.0
Total	500	100.0

Table 1.2: Age-wise distribution of the respondents

Age-Group	Frequency	Percent
21 to 30	141	28.2
31 to 40	187	37.4
41 to 45	172	34.4
Total	500	100.0

Table 1.3: Distribution of the respondents according to their educational qualifications

Educational level	Frequency	Percent
Illiterates	111	22.2
Primary Schooling	85	17.0
High Schooling	176	35.2
Graduates	128	25.6
Total	500	100.0

Table No 1.4: Occupational distribution of the respondents

Occupation	Frequency	Percent
Unorganized	188	37.6
Organized	107	21.4
Unemployed	205	41.0
Total	500	100.0

Table No 1.5: Distribution of the respondents by their monthly income

Economic Status	Frequency	Percent
<2000 ($43)	146	29.2
>2000-5000 ($43-107)	130	26.0
>5000 ($107-213)	224	44.8
Total	500	100.0

Table No 1.6: Distribution of the respondents by the nature of the Family

Nature of Family	Frequency	Percent
Nuclear	350	70.0
Joint	150	30.0
Total	500	100.0

Table No 1.7: Distribution of the respondents by area-wise

Area	Frequency	Percent
Rural	264	52.8
Urban	236	47.2
Total	500	100.0

TABLE NO 1.18: DISTRIBUTION OF THE RESPONDENTS BY TALUK—WISE

Taluk	Frequency	Percent
Dindigul	72	14.4
Kodaikanal	72	14.4
Natham	71	14.2
Nilakkottai	71	14.2
Oddanchatram	71	14.2
Palani	71	14.2
Vedasandur	72	14.4
Total	500	100.0

TABLE NO 1.9: DISTRIBUTION OF THE RESPONDENTS BY THEIR CASTE

Caste	Frequency	Percent
BC	161	32.2
MBC	215	43.1
SC	124	24.7
Total	500	100.0

TABLE NO 1.10: DISTRIBUTION OF THE RESPONDENTS BY THEIR FREQUENCY OF USE OF THE MEDIA

Frequency of Use of Media	Frequency	Percent
Daily	123	24.6
Once a Week	230	46.0
Rarely	147	29.4
Total	500	100.0

Table No 1.11: Distribution of the respondents according to their involvement in action-oriented groups

Member	Frequency	Percent
Yes	318	63.6
No	182	36.4
Total	500	100.0

Select Bibliography

Books

Abercrombie, Nicholas. "Knowledge, Order and Human Anatomy." In *Making Sense of Modern Times*, edited by James Hunter and Stephen Ainley. London: RKP, 1986.

Agarwal, Bina, ed. *Structures of Patriarchy*. New Delhi: Kali for Women, 1988.

Agarwal, S. Khurana . *Directory of Women's Studies in India*. New Delhi: AIU and the Common Wealth of Learning, 1991.

Arjunan, Narayan Kutty. *Psychology of Learning and Instruction*. Trivandrum: Atlanta Books, 2002.

Arnold, David. *Colonizing the Body: State, Medicine and Epidemic Disease in Nineteenth Century India*. New Delhi: Oxford University Press, 1993.

Atwood, Margaret. "The Female Body." In *The Female Body: Figures, Styles, Speculations*, edited by Laurence Goldstein. Ann Harbor, MI: The University of Michigan Press, 1991.

Bagwe, Anjali. *Of Woman Caste: The Experience of Gender in Rural India*. Calcutta: Stree, 1995.

Bande, Usha, and Atma Ram. *Woman in Indian Short Stories*. New Delhi: Rawat, 2003.

Bartky, Sandra Lee. "Foucault, Feminism and Patriarchal Power." In *Feminism and Foucault: Reflections on Resistance*, edited by Irene Diamond and Lee Quinby. Boston, Mass: Northeastern University Press, 1988.

———. *Femininity and Domination: Studies in the Phenomenology of Oppression*. New York: Routledge, 1990.

Beausoliel, Natalie. "Makeup in Everyday Life." In *Many Mirrors: Body Image and Social Relations*, edited by Nicole Sault. New Jersey: Rutgers University Press, 1994.

Bell, Catherine. *Ritual Theory, Ritual Practice*. New York: Oxford University Press, 1992.

Bennett, Lynn. *Dangerous Wives and Sacred Sisters: Social and Symbolic Roles of High Caste Women in Nepal*. New York: Columbia University Press, 1983.

Berger, John. *Ways of Seeing*. London: Penguin Books, 1988.

Bhasin, Kamala, and Nighat Said Khan. *Feminism in South Asia*. New Delhi: Kali for Women, 1986.

Bleier, Ruth. *Science and Gender: A Critique of Biology and its Theories on Women*. Oxford: Pergamon Press, 1984.

Bordo, Susan R., and Alison M. Jaggar, eds. *Gender/Body/Knowledge: Feminist Reconstructions of Being and Knowing*. New Brunswick, NJ: Rutgers University Press, 1989.

Bordo, Susan. "Reading the Slender Body." In *Women, Science and the Body Politic*, edited by M. Jacubus, E. Fox Keller and S. Shuttleworth. New York: Methuen, 1989.

———. *Unbearable Weight: Feminism, Western Culture, and the Body*. Berkeley: University of California Press, 1993.

Brook, Barbara. *Feminist Perspectives on the Body*. London; New York: Longman, 1999.

Brown, Peter. *The Body and Society. Men, Women, and Sexual Renunciation in Early Christianity*. New York: Columbia University Press, 1988.

Buckley, Thomas, and Alma Gottileb. *Blood Magic: The Anthropology of Menstruation*. Berkeley: University of California Press, 1988.

Bumiller, Elisabeth. *May You Be The Mother of a Hundred Sons*. New Delhi: Penguin Books, 1991.

Butler, Judith. *Gender Trouble: Feminism and the Subversion of Identity*. New York: Routledge, 1990.

———. *Bodies that Matter: On the Discursive Limits of Sex*. London: Routledge, 1994.

Bynum, Caroline Walker. *Fragmentation and Redemption: Essays on Gender and the Human Body in Medieval Religion*. New York: Zone Books, 1991.

Campbell, Joseph, ed. *Myths and Symbols in Indian Art and Civilization*. London: Pantheon Books, 1963.

Casagrande, Carla. "The Protected Woman." In *Silences of the Middle Ages*, edited by Christiane Klapisch-Zuber. USA: Harvard University Press, 1992.

Chopin, Kate. *The Awakening*. New York: Bandam Classics, 1981.

Conboy, Katie, et al., eds. *Writing on the Body: Female Embodiment and Feminist Theory*. New York: Columbia University Press, 1997.

Curran, Charles E., et al., eds. *Feminist Ethics and the Catholic Moral Tradition*. New York: Paulist Press, 1996.

Dange, Sindhu S. "Symbolism of the Ceremonial Rituals." In *Indian Symbology*, edited by Kirti Trivedi. Calcutta: Industrial Design Centre, 1987.

De Beauvoir, Simone. *The Second Sex*. Translated by H. M. Parshley. New York: Knopf, 1953.

Deshmukh, Joy–Ranadive. *Space for Power: Women's Work and Family Strategies in South and South-East Asia*. India: Rainbow Publishers in Collaboration with Centre for Women's Development Studies, 2002.

Deutsch, Helene. *The Psychology of Women*, Vol. 1. New York: Grune & Stratton, 1944.

Dietrich, Gabrielle. *Reflections on the Women's Movement, Religion, Ecology, Development*. New Delhi: Horizon Publications 1992.

Doniger, O'Flaherty. *Hindu Myths*. Harmondsworth: Penguin, 1975.

Doniger, Wendy, and Brain K. Smith, trans. *The Laws of Manu*. India: Penguin, 1992.

Douglas, Mary. *Purity and Danger: An Analysis of the Concepts of Pollution and Taboo*. London: RKP, 1966.

———. *Natural Symbols: Exploration in Cosmology*. London: The Cresset Press, 1970.

Durkheim, Emile. *Suicide: A Study in Sociology*. Glencoe, IL: Free Press, 1954.

Duroche, Leo. "Male Perception as a Social Construct." In *Men, Masculinities and Social Theory*, edited by Jeff Hearn and David H. Morgan. London: Hyman, 1990.

Edwards, John N. *The Family and Change*. New York: New York University Press, 1969.

Eisenstein, Hester. *Contemporary Feminist Thought*. London: Allen and Unwin, 1984.

Estes, Clarisa Pinkola. *Women Who Run With the Wolves*. New York: Ballantine, 1992.

Fausto-Sterling, Anne. *Myths of Gender: Biological Theories about Women and Men*. New York: Basic Books, 1985.

Featherstone, Shulamith. *The Dialectic of Sex*. New York: Bantam, 1971.

Foucault, Michel. "Body/Power." In *Michel Foucault: Power/ Knowledge*, edited by C. Gordon. Brighton: Harvester, 1980.

———. *Discipline and Punish: The Birth of the Prison*. Harmondsworth: Penguin, 1979.

———. *The History of Sexuality, vol. 1: An Introduction*. Harmondsworth: Penguin, 1981.

Friedan, Betty. *The Second Stage*. New York: Summit Books, 1981.

Gaines, Jane, and Charlotte Herzog, eds. *Fabrications: Costume and the Female Body*. New York: Routledge, 1990.

Game, Ann. *Undoing the Social: Towards a Deconstructive Sociology*. Milton Keynes: Open University Press, 1991.

Gandhi, Nandita, and Nandita Shah. *The Issues at Stake: Theory and practice in the Contemporary Women's Movement in India*. Delhi: Kali for Women, 1992.

Ganesh, Kamala. *Boundary Walls: Caste and Women in a Tamil Community*. Delhi: Hindustan Publications, 1993.

Geddes, Patrick, and Arthur Thomson. *The Evolution of Sex*. London: Walter Scott, 1889.

Germaine, Adrienne, and Rachel Kyte. *The Cairo Consciousness: The Right Agenda for the Right Time*. United Nations: International Women's Health Coalition, 1995.

Ghadially, Rehana, ed. *Women in Indian Society: A Reader*. New Delhi: Sage Publications, 1988.

Giddens, Anthony. *The Constitution of Society: Outline of the Theory of Structuration*. Berkeley: University of California Press, 1984.

Glaser, Barney, and Anselm Strauss. *The Discovery of Grounded Theory*. London: Sociology Press, 1967.

Goffman, Erving. *Gender Advertisement*. London: Macmillan, 1979.

———. *The Presentation of Self in Everyday Life*. Harmondsworth: Penguin, 1969.

———. "The arrangement between the sexes." In *Interaction*, edited by M. Deegan and M. Hill. Winchester, Mass: Allen and Unwin, 1987.

———. *Behaviour in Public Places: Notes on the Social Organization of Gatherings*. New York: The Free Press, 1963.

———. *Frame Analysis: An Essay on the Organization of Experience*. New York: Harper and Row, 1974.

———. *Stigma: Notes on the Management of Spoiled Identity*. Harmondsworth: Penguin, 1968.

Gokilvani, Raj. *Women's Studies: Principles, Theories and Methodologies*. Karaikudi: Alagappa University, 1999.

Goldstein, Laurence, ed. *The Female Body: Figures, Styles, Speculations*. Ann Harbor, MI: The University of Michigan Press, 1991.

Gore, M. S. *Urbanisation and Family Change*. Delhi: Rawat Publications, 1972.

Grosz, Elisabeth. *Volatile Bodies: Toward a Corporeal Feminism*. Bloomington: Indiana University Press, 1994.

Gudorf, Christine E. "Body, Self and Sexual Identity." In *Body and Sexuality*, edited by Agnes M. Brazil and Andrea Lizares Si. Quezon City: Ateneo de Manila University Press, 2007.

———. *Body, Sex and Pleasure: Reconstructing Christian Sexual Ethics*. Ohio: The Pilgrim Press, 2003.

Hartsock, Nancy. *Money, Sex, and Power: Toward a Feminist Historical Materialism*. New York: Long man, 1983.

Hastrup, Ki-sten. "The Semantics of Biology: Virginity." In *Defining Females*, edited by Shirley Ardener. London: Croom Helm, 1978.

Held, Virginia. *Feminist Morality: Transforming Culture, Society, and Politics*. Chicago: University of Chicago Press, 1993.

Henning, Michelle. "Don't Touch Me (I'm Electric): On Gender and Sensation in Modernity." In *Women's Bodies: Discipline and Transgression*, edited by Jane Arthurs and Jean Grimshaw. London: Cassell, 1999.

Hermann, Anne C., and Abigail J. Stewart, eds. *Theorising Feminism: Parallel Trends in the Humanities And Social Sciences,* 2nd ed. Boulder, CO: Westview, 2000.

Hoagland, Sarah Lucia. *Lesbian Ethics: Toward a New Value.* Palo Alto, CA: Institute of Lesbian Studies, 1988.

Isherwood, Lisa, ed. *The Good News of the Body: Sexual Theology and Feminism.* New York: New York University Press, 2000.

Jackson, Stevi, et al. *Women Studies: A Reader.* Whitesheaf: Hemel Hampestead Harvester, 1993.

Jackson, Stevi, and Jackie Jones, eds. *Contemporary Feminist Theories.* New York: New York University Press, 1998.

Jain, P.C., et al. *Scheduled Caste Women.* New Delhi: Rawat, 1997.

Jeffreys, Sheila. *Anticlimax: A Feminist Perspective on the Sexual Revolution.* London: Women's Press, 1990.

Jordanova, Ludmilla. *Sexual Visions: Images of Gender in Science and Medicine between the Eighteenth and Twentieth Centuries.* New York: Harvester Wheatsheaf, 1989.

Josseleson, Ruethellen. *Finding Herself: Pathways to Identity Development in Women.* Oxford: Jossey Bass Publishers, 1990.

Kakar, Sudhir. *Intimate Relations: Exploring Indian Sexuality.* New Delhi: Penguin, 1989.

Kane, P.V. *History of Dharmasastras.* Calcutta: Penguin, 1967.

Kaplan, Gisela, and Lesley Rogers. "The definition of male and female: Biological reductionism and the sanctions of Normality." In *Feminist Knowledge, Critique and Construct*, edited by Sneja Gunew. London: Routledge, 1990.

Kapur, Promilla. *Love, Marriage, Sex and the Indian Woman.* New Delhi: Orient Paperbacks, 1976.

Krishnan, Rajam. K lam T‡rum PeЇmai (Women through the years). Chennai: Tamil Puthahalayam, 2000.

Kudchedkar, Shirin, and Sabiha Al-Issar, ed. *Violence against Women: Women against Violence.* New Delhi: Pencraft International, 1998.

Kuhn, Annette. *The Power of the Image: Essays in Representation and Sexuality.* London: Routledge & Kegan Paul, 1985.

Laqueur, Thomas. "Orgasm, Generation, and the Politics of Reproductive Biology." In *The Making of the Modern Body: Sexuality and Society in the Nineteenth Century,* edited by C. Gallagher and Thomas Laqueur. Berkeley, CA: University of California press, 1987.

Leonardo, Micaela Di. *Gender at the Crossroads of Knowledge: Feminist Anthropology in the Post-Modern Era.* Berkeley: University of California Press, 1991.

Levinson, David, and Melvin Ember. *Encyclopedia of Cultural Anthropology.* New York: Henry Holt & Co., 1996.

Magtoto, Liza C. *Birthings: A Journal of Shared Lives* (A Nationwide Information Tour on Women's Health and Reproductive Rights). Quezon City: PETA, 2002.

Malhotra, Anju, et al. "Measuring Women's Empowerment as a Variable in International Development." 2002. Unpublished paper prepared for the World Bank.

Malone, Mary T. *Women & Christianity.* New York: Orbis, 2001.

Mandelbaum, David. *Women's Seclusion and Men's Honour.* Tuscon: The University of Arizona Press, 1988.

Moi, Toril. *Sexual / Textual Politics: Feminist Literary Theory*. London: Methuen, 1985.

Montagu, Ashley. *The Natural Superiority of Women*. London: Altamira, 2005.

Morgen, Sandra, ed. *Gender and Anthropology: Critical Reviews for Research and Teaching*. Washington, D.C.: AAA. 1989.

Mowli, V. Chandra, ed. *Role of Voluntary Organizations in Social Development*. New Delhi: Sterling Publishers Pvt. Ltd., 1990.

Nabar, Vrinda. *Caste as Woman*. Calcutta: Penguin, 1995.

Niranjana, Seemanthini. "Femininity, Space and the Female Body: An Anthropological Perspective." In *Embodiment: Essays on Gender and Identity*, edited by M. Thapan, 107–124. Delhi: Oxford University Press, 1997.

———. *Gender and Space*. New Delhi: Sage, 2001.

Norris, Pippa. *Politics & Sexual Equality*. Boulder, Colorado: Lynne Rienner, 1987.

O'Hanlon, Rosalind. "Issues of Widowhood: Gender and Resistance in Colonial Western India." In *Contesting Power: Resistance and Everyday Social relations in South Asia*, edited by Douglas E. Haynes and Gyan Prakash. Berkeley: University of California Press, 1991.

Orbach, Suzie. *Fat is a Feminist issue*. London: Arrow Books, 1988.

Padma, Vathi A.S. Peṇ Moḻi (The Language of a Woman). Chennai: Sekhar Pathipagam, 2001.

Paris, Bernard J. *Imagined Human Beings*. New York: New York University Press, 1997.

Periannan, Sebastian. *Social Research Methodology: An Introduction*. Chennai: University Of Madras, 2003.

Plaskow, Judith. "Embodiment and Ambivalence: A Jewish Feminist Perspective in Embodiment, Morality, and Medicine." In *Theology and Medicine*, edited by Lisa Sowle Cahill and Margaret A. Farley. London: Kluwer Academic Publishers.

Porter, I. James. ed. *Constructions of the Classical Body*. Ann Arbor, MI: The University of Michigan Press, 1999.

Pui-lan, Kwok. Introducing Asian Feminist Theology. Sheffield: Sheffield Academic Press, 2000.

Rahner, Karl. Theological Investigations, Vol. 9. London: Darton, Longman & Todd, 1972.

Raj, Iruthaya. Dindigul Anna District at a Glance. Dindigul: Unpublished Manuscript, 1995.

Ram, Kalpana. Mukkuvar Women: Gender, Hegemony and Capitalist Transformation in A South Indian Fishing Community. Delhi: Kali for Women, 1992.

Ramazanoglu, Caroline, and Janet Holland. Feminist Methodology: Challenges and Choices. London: Sage, 2002.

Rao, Vijayeswari. *Women and Society*. Mumbai: Himalaya, 2004.

Raphael, M. *Theology and Embodiment: The Post-Patriarchal Reconstruction of Female Sacrality*. Sheffield England: Sheffield Academic Press, 1996.

Rector, Lallene J. "Are We Making Love Yet?: Theological And Psychological Perspectives on the Role of gender Identity in the Experience of Domination." In *The Good News of the Body: Sexual Theology and Feminism*, edited by Lisa Isherwood. New York: New York University Press, 2000.

Reiter, Rayna, ed. Toward an Anthropology of Women. New York: Monthly Review Press, 1975.

Rich, Adrienne. Of Woman Born: Motherhood as Experience and Institution. New York: WW Norton and Company Inc., 1976.

Rosaldo, Michelle, and Louise Lamphere, eds. Women, Culture, and Society. Stanford: Stanford University Press, 1974.

———. "The Trouble with Patriarchy." In *No Turning Back: Writing from the Women's Liberation Movement 1975–80*. London: The Woman's Press, 1981.

Roy, Arundati. *The God of Small Things*. New Delhi: India Ink, 1997.

Rubin Suleiman, Susan. *The Female Body in Western Culture: Contemporary Perspectives*. Cambridge: Harvard University Press, 1986.

Ruether, Rosemary Radford. "Sex in the Catholic Tradition." In *The Good News of the Body: Sexual Theology and Feminism*, edited by Lisa Isherwood. New York: New York University Press, 2000.

Russel, Bernard. *Research Methods in Anthropology: Qualitative and Quantitative Approaches*. London: Altamira Press, 1995.

Russel, Diana E. H. *The Secret Trauma: Incest in the Lives of Girls and Women*. New York: Basic Books, 1988.

Russel, Letty M., and J. Shannon, ed. *The Dictionary of Feminist Theology*. Mowbray: Westminster, JohnKnox Press, 1996.

Saivings, Valerie. "Human Situation: A Feminine View." In *Woman Spirit Rising: A Feminist Reader in Religion*, edited by Carol Christ and Judith Plaskow. New York: Harper and Row Books, 1979.

Sarkar, Tanika *Hindu Wife, Hindu Nation: Community, Religion and Cultural Nationalism*. New Delhi: Permanent Black, 2001.

Schneiders, Sandra. *Beyond Patching: Faith and Feminism in the Catholic Church*. New York: Paulist, 1991.

Scott, James E. *The Weapons of the Weak: Everyday Forms of Peasant Resistance*. London: Yale University Press, 1985.

Shanthi, Margaret. "The Impact of Tanneries on Women Workers and Environment." In *Ecology: A Theological Response*, edited by Andreas Nehring. Madras: The Gurukul Summer Institute, 1993.

Shilling, Chris. *The Body and Social Theory*. London: Sage, 1993.

Shirwadkar, Swati. *Women and Socio-Cultural Changes*. New Delhi: Gyan Publishing House, 1998.

Shiva, Vandana. *Close to Home: Women Reconnect Ecology, Health and Development*. London: Earthscan Publications, 1994.

Shulman, David Dean. *Tamil Temple Myths*. Princeton: University Press, 1980.

Soundariya, Hilaria. "Rural Dalit and Self Help Groups." PhD diss., Gandhi Gram Deemed University, 2004.

Spacks, Patricia Meyer. *The Female Imagination*. New York: Norton, 1975.

Srivastava, Sharad. *The New Woman in Indian English Fiction*. New Delhi: Creative Books, 1996.

Stanley, Liz, and Sue Wise, ed. *Breaking out Feminist Consciousness and Feminist Research*. London: Routledge & Kegan Paul, 1983.

Strauss, Anselm. *Qualitative Analysis for Social Scientists*. Cambridge, England: Cambridge University Press, 1987.

Strauss, Anselm, and Juliet Corbin. *Basics of Qualitative Research: Grounded Theory Procedures and Techniques*. London: Sage, 1990.

Strauss, Levi. *The Elementary Structures of Kinship*. Boston: Beacon Press, 1969.

Suleiman, Susan Rubin. *The Female Body in Western Culture*. Cambridge: Harvard University Press, 1986.

Synnott, Anthony. *The Body Social. Symbolism, Self and Society*. London: New York: Routledge, 1994.

Thapan, Meenakshi, ed. *Embodiment: Essays on Gender and Identity*. Delhi: Oxford University Press, 1997.

Thatcher, Adrian, and Elisabeth Stuart, eds. *Christian Perspectives on Sexuality and Gender*. Grand Rapids: Wm B Eerdmans Publishing Co, 1996.

The Boston Women's Health Book Collective, *The NEW Our Bodies, Ourselves*. New York: Simon and Schuster, Inc., 1984.

Thilkavathi, IPS. Cinimāvukku Cila Kēḷvikaḷ (Some Questions to Cinema). Dindigul: Vaiharai Pathipagam, 2000.

Turner, Bryan S. *Religion and Social Theory*. London: Heinemann Educational Books, 1983.

Wadley, Susan S., ed. *The Powers of Tamil Women*. New Delhi: Manohar, 1991.

Westkott, Marcia. *The Feminist Legacy of Karen Horney*. New Haven: Yale University Press, 1986.

Widge, Anjali. "Patriarchy, Social Control and the Female Body." In *The Family in a Changing World*, edited by Rudolf C. Heredia. New Delhi: Indian Social Institute, 1995.

Wilfred, Felix. *On the Banks of Ganges*. Delhi: Indian Society for Promoting Christian Knowledge, 2005.

———. *The Sling of Utopia*. Delhi: ISPCK, 2005.

Wolf, Naomi. *The Beauty Myth: How Images of Beauty Are Used Against Women*. New York: Harper Collins Publishers, 2002.

Woolf, Virginia. *A Room of One's Own*. New York: Harcourt Brace Jovanovich, 1957.

Young, Lola. "Racializing Femininity." In *Women's Bodies: Discipline and Transgression*, edited by Jane Arthurs and Jean Grimshaw, 67–86. New York: Cassell, 1999.

Young, Pauline V. *Scientific Social Survey and Research*. New York: Prentice Hall, 1994.

Articles

Ammicht Quinn, Regina. "Body Culture, Christian Culture and Ethics: An Exercise in Ambivalence." Private circulation (2002) 1–10.

Baber, Zaheer. "Beyond the Structure/Agency Dualism: An Evaluation of Gidden's Theory of Structuration." *Sociological Inquiry* 61 (2/1991) 219–30.

Basu, Soma. "Pillow Rock." *The Hindu-Metro Plus* (April 2, 2005) 1.

Bechtle, Regina. "Theological Trends: Feminist Approaches to Theology 1." *The Way* 27 (April 1987) 124.

Berger, Teresa. "Woman as Alien Bodies in the Body of Christ? The Place of Women in Worship." *Concilium* (3/1995) 112–20.

Berthelot, Jacques. "Sociological Discourse and the Body" *Theory Culture and Society* 3 (1986) 155–64.

Bourdieu, Pierre. "The Social Space and the Genesis of Groups." *Theory and Society* 14 (6/1985) 723–44.

Cattin, Yves. "Human Beings Cross Frontiers." *Concilium* 2 (1992) 5.

Doctor, Geeta. "In the Garb of Modesty?" *The Hindu–Magazine* (October 9, 2005) 1.

Doshi, Tishani. "Myth of Motherhood." *The Hindu, Sunday Magazine* (November 23, 2003) 4.

Gelfant, Blanche. "Sister to Faust: The City's 'Hungry' Woman as Heroine." *Novel: Forum on Fiction*, 15/1 (1981) 23–38.

Goffman, Erving. "The Arrangement between the Sexes." *Theory and Society* 4 (1977) 301–31.

———. "The interaction order." *American Sociological Review* 48 (1983) 213–45.

Halkes, Catherina. "Feminist Theology: An Interim Assessment." *Concilium* 134 (4/1980) 110–23.

Hegde, Radha S. "Sons and Mothers: Framing the maternal Body and the Politics of Reproduction in South Indian Context." *Women's Studies in Communication*, 22/1 (1999) 22–28.

Jeyaseeli, Beulah. "Gender Based Crimes in Tamilnadu in 2000: Some Issues and Implications." *Journal of Gender and Progress* 1 (2003)112–15.

Kala, Chitra. "Beyond the Bed." Outlook (November 24, 2003) 40.

Kapoor, Deepti. "Single & Swinging." *The Week* (February 27, 2005) 41–42.

Kishor, Sunita, and Kamala Gupta. "Women's Empowerment in India and Its States: Evidence from the NFHS." *Economical and Political Weekly* (February 14–20, 2004) 694–712.

Menne, Ferdinand. "Catholic Sexual Ethics and Gender Roles in the Church." Concilium 134 (4/1980)14–25.

Nambath, Suresh. "A Freedom at Stake . . ." *The Hindu-Sunday Magazine* (November 27, 2005) 1.

Nandal, Santosh. "Laws Inadequate to Check Atrocities on Women." *Women's Link* 10 (April–June 2/2004) 34–37.

Pui-lan, Kwok. "Reflection of Women's Sacred Scriptures." *Concilium* (3/1998) 105–12.

Reuther, Rosemary Radford. "Re-evaluating the Body in Eco-Feminism." *Concilium* (2/2002) 41–49.

Runkle, Susan. "The Beauty Obsession." *Manushi* 145 (Nov–Dec, 2004) 10–11.

Sail, Shashi. "Witch Hunting in the 21st Century." *Women's Link* 9 (2003) 45–47.

Shirin, Baba. "Wombs as Battlegrounds." *Mainstream* Vol. XLII, 20 (May 8, 2004) 22–24.

Sinaga, Debora Purada."Women Claiming Healing and Cure: A Reflection on Mark 5:25–34." *In God's Image* 22 (2003) 12–4.

Siwal, B Rao "Women's Movement in India." *Women's Link* Vol.11, No.2 (April–June 2005) 4–7.

Wong, Lai Fan. "Menstruation & Women's Spirituality." *In God's Image* 22 (2003) 6–7.

Young, Iris. "Throwing like a Girl: A Phenomenology of Feminine Body Comportment, Motility, and Spatiality." *Human Studies* 3 (1980) 137–56.

Documents

Census Handbook 1951—Madurai District. Madras: The Superintendent Government Press, 1953.

Tamilnadu-An Economic Appraisal 2001-2002: Department of Evaluation and Applied Research Government of Tamilnadu. Chennai: Kuralagam, 2002.

United Nations (1995): Population and Development: Programme of Action Adopted at the International Conference on Population and Development, Cairo. September 5–13, 1994, Department for Economics and Social Information and Policy Analysis, United Nations.

Women in Tamilnadu-A Profile. Chennai: Department of Women's Welfare—The Tamilnadu Corporation for Development of Women Limited Madras, 1981.

www.ingramcontent.com/pod-product-compliance
Lightning Source LLC
Chambersburg PA
CBHW051931160426
43198CB00012B/2113